FIX-IT and FORGET-IT®
Plant-Based
KETO
Cookbook

Healthy and Delicious Low-Carb, Vegan Recipes

HOPE COMERFORD

Good Books

New York, New York

Good Books books may be purchased in bulk at special discounts for sales promotion, corporate gifts, fund-raising, or educational purposes. Special editions can also be created to specifications. For details, contact the Special Sales Department, Good Books, 307 West 36th Street, 11th Floor, New York, NY 10018 or info@skyhorsepublishing.com.

Good Books is an imprint of Skyhorse Publishing, Inc.®, a Delaware corporation.

Visit our website at www.goodbooks.com.

10 9 8 7 6 5 4 3

Library of Congress Cataloging-in-Publication Data is available on file.

Cover design by Daniel Brount
Cover photo by Bonnie Matthews

Print ISBN: 978-1-68099-614-2
Ebook ISBN: 978-1-68099-635-7

Printed in China

Contents

Welcome to *Fix-It and Forget-It Plant-Based Keto Cookbook*

If you're following a plant-based keto diet, then this book is going to be your new best friend! Fix-It and Forget-It Plant-Based Keto Cookbook contains sixty slow-cooker and an additional forty bonus non–slow cooker recipes, which all adhere to plant-based food guidelines, while also fitting within keto guidelines.

We're bringing you breakfasts like Tofu Scrambles and Tofu Cinnamon Toast with Coconut Cream, savory soups like Tofutilla Soup, delicious dinners like Blueberry & Tofu Salad and Tempeh Cacciatore, and even amazing desserts like Crispy Tofu with Toasted Coconut and Warm Strawberry Compote! Is your mouth watering yet? If not, it should be!

As you begin journeying through this book, I always suggest reading from cover to cover. I can't tell you the good recipes I've missed in the past by not following this advice. Don't become overwhelmed. Bookmark or dog-ear the pages of the recipes that interest you the most as you go through. Then, when you've looked at everything, go back to those marked pages and pick two to three to start with. You may even consider choosing a recipe or two for which you already have the ingredients on hand. If not, start that grocery list and get to your local store and grab only what you need. Staying within plant-based keto guidelines can seem like a daunting task. Our hope is this book takes that worry and replaces it with tools for success and deliciousness!

What Is a Plant-Based Keto Diet?

A plant-based diet is one that involves eating whole, real foods that come from plants. A keto diet involves eating foods high in fat and low in carbs. By lowering the level of carbs you are eating and increasing the amount of fat you're eating to replace the carbs, your body starts to go into a metabolic state known as ketosis.

It is also said that by following a keto diet, your blood sugar and insulin levels decrease dramatically. Many believe there are some major health benefits to achieve by following this diet, including weight loss. Many believe by following a plant-based diet, you can lower your risk of obesity and other chronic diseases. Some also simply follow a plant-based diet to eliminate the use of animal products altogether and eliminate the use of processed foods.

What makes this combination a bit trickier is, on a normal plant-based diet, you would consume a lot of whole grains, legumes, and all kinds of fruits and vegetables. On a normal keto diet, you would consume full-fat dairy and unprocessed meats. When you pair plant-based with keto, it removes all whole grains, legumes, dairy, meat, and many fruits and vegetables. Therefore, it gives you fewer foods to choose from.

In this book, you will find most protein replaced by tofu or tempeh, as seitan, another popular plant-based protein choice, is made with wheat gluten. You may discover many new or favorite plant-based dairy substitutes. With the keto diet also being a no-sugar diet, you will find several natural (plant-based) sweeteners recommended throughout the book in various recipes.

As always, it is recommended that you consult your physician before beginning any diet to make sure it is the right choice for you. If you choose to follow this diet, we hope you have great success and that this book helps you along your journey.

Plant Based–Keto Friendly Foods

*Foods marked with this symbol are to be used sparingly because they are higher in carbs.

Vegetables	Fruits
• Artichoke hearts	• Avocados
• Asparagus	• Blueberries
• Beets*	• Coconut
• Bell peppers	• Cranberries (fresh only)
• Bok choy	• Lemon
• Broccoli	• Lime
• Brussels sprouts *	• Raspberries
• Cabbage	• Strawberries
• Cauliflower	• Tomatoes
• Celery	**Nuts**
• Cucumbers	• Almonds
• Eggplant	• Brazil nuts
• Fennel	• Cashews *
• Garlic	• Hazelnuts
• Kale	• Macadamia nuts
• Leafy greens	• Peanuts
• Microgreens	• Pecans
• Mushrooms	• Pistachios *
• Okra	• Walnuts
• Onion	**Nut Butters**
• Radishes	• Almond butter
• Shallots	• Cashew butter *
• Sprouts of all kinds	• Coconut butter
• Zucchini	• Hazelnut butter
	• Macadamia nut butter

Oils	Seeds
• Almond oil	• Chia seeds
• Avocado oil	• Flaxseed
• Coconut oil	• Hemp seeds
• Flaxseed oil	• Pumpkin seeds
• Hazelnut oil	• Sunflower seeds
• Macadamia nut oil	**Sauces/Condiments**
• MCT oil	• Apple cider vinegar
• Olive oil	• Balsamic vinegar (vegan)
• Walnut oil	• Chili sauce
Proteins	• Coconut aminos & liquid aminos
• Tempeh	• Hot sauce
• Tofu	• Hummus *
Refrigerated Staples	• Fresh salsa
• Dairy-free cheese	• Mustard
• Dairy-free milk	• Rice vinegar
• Dairy-free yogurt	• Tamari
• Pickles (watch for sugar)	• Tomato sauce
• Vegan butter	• White vinegar
• Vegan cream cheese	**Pantry Staples**
Other Staples	• Baking powder
• Black soybeans	• Baking soda
• Edamame	• Cacao nibs
• Herbs and spices	• Coconut flour
• Kelp flakes	• Coconut milk (canned, full fat)
• Kelp noodles	• Cocoa or cacao powder
• Lupini beans	• Dark chocolate (85% or higher)
• Nori sheets	• Hearts of palm
• Roasted seaweed	• Jackfruit
• Peanut butter	• Nutritional yeast
• Pecan butter	• Psyllium husk
• Shirataki noodles	• Vanilla extract (no sugar added)
• Sunflower seed butter	
• Tahini	

Choosing a Slow Cooker

Not all slow cookers are created equal . . . or work equally as well for everyone!

Those of us who use slow cookers frequently know we have our own preferences when it comes to which slow cooker we choose to use. For instance, I love my programmable slow cooker, but there are many programmable slow cookers I've tried that I've strongly disliked. Why? Because some go by increments of 15 or 30 minutes and some go by 4, 6, 8, or 10 hours. I dislike those restrictions, but I have family and friends who don't mind them at all! I am also pretty brand loyal when it comes to my manual slow cookers because I've had great success with those and have had unsuccessful moments with slow cookers of other brands. So, which slow cooker(s) is/are best for your household?

It really depends on how many people you're feeding and if you're gone for long periods of time. Here are my recommendations:

For 2–3 person household	3–5 quart slow cooker
For 4–5 person household	5–6 quart slow cooker
For a 6+ person household	6½–7 quart slow cooker

Large slow cooker advantages/disadvantages:

Advantages:
- You can fit a loaf pan or a baking dish into a 6- or 7-quart, depending on the shape of your cooker. That allows you to make bread or cakes, or even smaller quantities of main dishes. (Take your favorite baking dish and loaf pan along when you shop for a cooker to make sure they'll fit inside.)
- You can feed large groups of people, or make larger quantities of food, allowing for leftovers, or meals, to freeze.

Disadvantages:
- They take up more storage room.
- They don't fit as neatly into a dishwasher.
- If your crock isn't ⅔–¾ full, you may burn your food.

Small slow cooker advantages/disadvantages:

Advantages:
- They're great for lots of appetizers, for serving hot drinks, for baking cakes straight in the crock, and for dorm rooms or apartments.
- Great option for making recipes of smaller quantities.

Disadvantages:
- Food in smaller quantities tends to cook more quickly than larger amounts. So keep an eye on it.
- Chances are, you won't have many leftovers. So, if you like to have leftovers, a smaller slow cooker may not be a good option for you.

My recommendation:

Have at least two slow cookers; one around 3 to 4 quarts and one 6 quarts or larger. A third would be a huge bonus (and a great advantage to your cooking repertoire!). The advantage of having at least a couple is you can make a larger variety of recipes. Also, you can make at least two or three dishes at once for a whole meal.

Manual vs. Programmable

If you are gone for only six to eight hours a day, a manual slow cooker might be just fine for you. If you are gone for more than eight hours during the day, I would highly recommend purchasing a programmable slow cooker that will switch to warm when the cook time you set is up. It will allow you to cook a wider variety of recipes.

The two I use most frequently are my 4-quart manual slow cooker and my 6½-quart programmable slow cooker. I like that I can make smaller portions in my 4-quart slow cooker on days I don't need or want leftovers, but I also love how my 6½-quart slow cooker can accommodate whole chickens, turkey breasts, hams, or big batches of soups. I use them both often.

Get to know your slow cooker . . .

Plan a little time to get acquainted with your slow cooker. Each slow cooker has its own personality—just like your oven (and your car). Plus, many new slow cookers cook hotter and faster than earlier models. I think that with all of the concern for food safety, the slow-cooker manufacturers have amped up their settings so that "High," "Low," and "Warm" are all higher temperatures than in the older models. That means they cook hotter—and therefore, faster—than the first slow cookers. The beauty of these little machines is that they're supposed to cook low and slow. We count on that when we flip the switch in the morning before we leave the house for ten hours or so. So, because none of us knows what kind of temperament our slow cooker has until we try it out, nor how hot it cooks, don't assume anything. Save yourself a disappointment and make the first recipe in your new slow cooker on a day when you're at home. Cook it for the shortest amount of time the recipe indicates. Then, check the food to see if it's done. Or if you start smelling food that seems to be finished, turn off the cooker and rescue your food.

Also, all slow cookers seem to have a "hot spot," which is of great importance to know, especially when baking with your slow cooker. This spot may tend to burn food in that area if you're not careful. If you're baking directly in your slow cooker, I recommend covering the "hot spot" with some foil.

Take notes . . .

Don't be afraid to make notes in your cookbook. It's yours! Chances are, it will eventually get passed down to someone in your family and they will love and appreciate all of your musings. Take note of which slow cooker you used and exactly how long it took to cook the recipe. The next time you make it, you won't need to try to remember. Apply what you learned to the next recipes you make in your cooker. If another recipe says it needs to cook 7–9 hours, and you've discovered your slow cooker cooks on the faster side, cook that recipe for 6–6½ hours and then check it. You can always cook a recipe longer—but you can't reverse things if it's overdone.

Get creative . . .

If you know your morning is going to be hectic, prepare everything the night before, take it out so the crock warms up to room temperature when you first get up in the morning, then plug it in and turn it on as you're leaving the house.

If you want to make something that has a short cook time and you're going to be gone longer than that, cook it the night before and refrigerate it for the next day. Warm it up when you get home. Or, cook those recipes on the weekend when you know you'll be home and eat them later in the week.

Slow-Cooking Tips & Tricks and Other Things You May Not Know

- Slow cookers tend to work best when they're ⅔ to ¾ of the way full. You may need to increase the cooking time if you've exceeded that amount, or reduce it if you've put in less than that. If you're going to exceed that limit, it would be best to reduce the recipe, or split it between two slow cookers. (Remember how I suggested owning at least two or three slow cookers?)

- Keep the lid on! Every time you take a peek, you lose 20 minutes of cooking time. Please take this into consideration each time you lift the lid! I know, some of you can't help yourself and are going to lift anyway. Just don't forget to tack on 20 minutes to your cook time for each time you peeked!

- Sometimes it's beneficial to remove the lid. If you'd like your dish to thicken a bit, take the lid off during the last half hour to hour of cooking time.

- If you have a big slow cooker (7- to 8-quart), you can cook a small batch in it by putting the recipe ingredients into an oven-safe baking dish or baking pan and then placing that into the cooker's crock. First, put a trivet or some metal jar rings on the bottom of the crock, and then set your dish or pan on top of them. Or a loaf pan may "hook onto" the top ridges of the crock belonging to a large oval cooker and hang there straight and securely, "baking" a cake or quick bread. Cover the cooker and flip it on.

- The outside of your slow cooker will be hot! Please remember to keep it out of reach of children and keep that in mind for yourself as well!

- Add fresh herbs 10 minutes before the end of the cooking time to maximize their flavor.

- If your recipe calls for sour cream or cream, stir it in 5 minutes before the end of the cooking time. You want it to heat but not boil or simmer.

Approximate Slow-Cooker Temperatures (Remember, each slow cooker is different):

- High—212°F–300°F
- Low—170°F–200°F
- Simmer—185°F
- Warm—165°F

This book includes more than just slow-cooker recipes! You'll also find recipes to be made on the stovetop, in the oven, or chilled in the refrigerator. An icon on the top right of each recipe page will give you that info at a glance. Recipes that can be whipped up in a matter of minutes without cooking, baking, or chilling are labeled "Quick & Easy."

Breakfast

Blueberry-Pomegranate Smoothie

Dena Tompkins
Huntersville, NC

Makes 2 servings
Prep. Time: 10 minutes

I cup nondairy milk of your choice

I cup fresh or frozen blueberries

Seeds from I small-medium pomegranate

I Tbsp. lemon juice

I Tbsp. vegan honey

6–8 ice cubes (if using frozen berries omit ice cubes)

1. Combine all ingredients except ice cubes in blender. Blend well.

2. Gradually add ice cubes (unless using frozen berries). Continue blending until smooth enough to draw up with straw.

TIP

Add some silken tofu for added protein.

Calories 211

Fat 3

Sodium 98

Carbs 47

Sugar 35

Protein 4

Berry Good Breakfast

Hope Comerford
Clinton Township, MI

Makes 2 servings
Prep. Time: 10 minutes

¼ cup blueberries

¼ cup raspberries

½ cup strawberries, diced

2 Tbsp. chopped almonds

2 Tbsp. chopped walnuts

2 Tbsp. chopped pecans

1 cup nondairy, plain yogurt of your choice

Drizzle of vegan honey

1. Mix the berries and nuts together.

2. Stir them into the yogurt.

3. Drizzle with a bit of vegan honey. Serve immediately.

Calories 344
Fat 25
Sodium 83
Carbs 24
Sugar 17
Protein 11

Smoothie Bowl

Hope Comerford
Clinton Township, MI

Makes 2 servings
Prep. Time: 10 minutes

⅓ cup frozen raspberries

⅓ cup frozen blueberries

⅓ cup frozen strawberries

1 medium avocado

2 Tbsp. full-fat canned coconut milk

2 Tbsp. plain coconut yogurt

1 scoop vanilla protein powder

Optional toppings:

Flaxseed

Toasted coconut

Cacao nibs

Warmed almond butter

1. Place the frozen raspberries, blueberries, strawberries, avocado, coconut milk, coconut yogurt, and protein powder into a blender. Blend until smooth.

2. Divide contents of blender between 2 bowls. Sprinkle with any of the optional toppings or other keto/plant-based toppings you wish.

TIP

Smoothie bowls can be made in a variety of ways, using a variety of other ingredients. Choose those that best suit your preferences. Experiment and have fun with them!

Calories 256

Fat 18

Sodium 9

Carbs 23

Sugar 9

Protein 5

Chia Breakfast Pudding

Hope Comerford
Clinton Township, MI

Makes 1 serving
Prep. Time: 23 minutes & *Refrigeration Time: 2 hours to overnight (depending on thickness you like)*

1 cup unsweetened almond, cashew, or coconut milk

3–4 Tbsp. chia seeds

½ Tbsp. vegan honey

¼ tsp. no-sugar-added vanilla extract

Optional mix-ins:

Your favorite no-sugar-added nut butter

Cacao powder or nibs

Sliced strawberries, blueberries, blackberries, or raspberries

Unsweetened coconut flakes

1. Mix together your milk of choice with the chia seeds, honey, and vanilla. At this time, you can mix in the nut butter or cacao powder if you're adding those. Place in the refrigerator for 20 minutes.

2. Stir your mixture again to break up any clumps. Place back in the refrigerator.

3. Let your pudding sit in the refrigerator for 2 hours, or overnight.

4. When you're ready to serve, you can mix in the cacao nibs, berries, or coconut flakes if you wish to add those.

Calories 212
Fat 12
Sodium 191
Carbs 22
Sugar 9
Protein 6

Tofu Cinnamon Toast with Coconut Cream

STOVETOP

Maria Shevlin
Sicklerville, NJ

Makes 4–6 servings
Prep. Time: 45 minutes ⚹ Cooking Time: 10–15 minutes

14–16-oz. block extra-firm tofu

Coconut oil for frying

3 Tbsp. stevia, *divided*

2 Tbsp. cinnamon

1 vanilla bean

1 (13½-oz.) can full-fat coconut milk, refrigerated for 24 hours

1. Press tofu with a towel wrapped around it and heavy object on top for 15 minutes to remove moisture.

2. Cut tofu into slices.

3. Fry in coconut oil until lightly browned.

4. Mix 2 Tbsp. stevia and cinnamon together and pour onto a plate. Coat both sides of each slice of tofu with this mixture.

5. Scoop the coconut cream off the top of the can and place in a metal bowl.

6. Halve the vanilla bean and scrape the seeds. Add to the coconut cream.

7. Whip the coconut cream with remaining stevia and vanilla bean until they form stiff peaks.

8. Serve each slice of cinnamon/stevia covered tofu with a generous dollop of whipped coconut cream.

Serving suggestion:
Serve with chiffonaded mint leaves atop for a refreshing dessert.

TIP
You could also add cocoa powder to the coconut cream instead of vanilla bean for a delicious chocolate topping.

Calories 880
Fat 77
Sodium 178
Carbs 17
Sugar 14
Protein 14

Avocado Breakfast Bowl

Maria Shevlin
Sicklerville, NJ

Makes 1 serving
Prep. Time: 10–15 minutes & Cooking Time: 5 minutes

1 semi-firm avocado, cut in half, peeled, and pitted

½ tsp. vegan butter, *divided*

2 Tbsp. Daiya brand shredded cheese of your choice, *divided*

Salt to taste

Pepper to taste

1 strip vegan bacon, crumbled

Green onion, *optional*

1. Place the avocado halves in a microwave-safe bowl or on a microwave-safe plate.

2. Add ¼ tsp. of vegan butter to each avocado well.

3. Add 1 Tbsp. of Daiya brand cheese to each avocado.

4. Add salt and pepper to taste on each avocado half.

5. Place the avocados in the microwave for 60–90 seconds. Remove.

6. Cook a slice of the vegan bacon and crumble it evenly over the halves.

7. Top with optional green onion, if desired.

Serving suggestion:

This would also be delicious with homemade vegan sour cream.

Calories 443
Fat 36
Sodium 283
Carbs 27
Sugar 7 Protein 9

Vegan Breakfast Scramble

Maria Shevlin
Sickerville, NJ

Makes 2 servings
Prep. Time: 10 minutes 🎋 Cooking Time: 25 minutes

I tsp. vegan butter, *divided*

1 (14–16 oz.) package firm tofu, crumbled

2 Tbsp. Daiya brand shredded cheese of your choice

Salt to taste

Pepper to taste

1–2 tsp. nutritional yeast

1. Add the vegan butter to a nonstick pan.

2. Add the crumbled tofu and cook until warmed.

3. Add the Daiya brand cheese and mix well.

4. Add the salt and pepper to taste. Remove from pan.

5. Divide the scramble evenly between two plates; sprinkle with the nutritional yeast.

Serving suggestion:

Serve each portion with a slice of vegan bacon, if desired.

TIP
This would make more servings if you added diced onion, diced bell peppers, and mushrooms for a delicious loaded veggie scramble.

Calories 228
Fat 14
Sodium 103
Carbs 8
Sugar 0
Protein 20

Tofu Scramble

Hope Comerford
Clinton Township, MI

Makes 4 servings
Prep. Time: 10 minutes plus pressing time ⚹ *Cooking Time: 3 hours* ⚹ *Ideal slow-cooker size: 3-qt.*

1 Tbsp. olive oil

1 (16-oz.) package extra-firm tofu, pressed and crumbled

2 cloves garlic, minced

3 Tbsp. minced shallots

1 Tbsp. fresh lemon juice

1 Tbsp. nutritional yeast

1 tsp. turmeric

½ tsp. salt

⅛ tsp. pepper

1. Use the olive oil to grease the inside of the crock.

2. Gently mix together all of the remaining ingredients in the crock.

3. Cover and cook on Low for 3 hours.

Serving suggestion:

Serve alongside vegan bacon strips and fresh berries.

Calories 137
Fat 8
Sodium 256
Carbs 5
Sugar 1
Protein 12

Mexican Breakfast Bowl

STOVETOP

Maria Shevlin
Sicklerville, NJ

Makes 4 servings
Prep. Time: Under 60 minutes ⚭ Cooking Time: 15 minutes

½ medium onion, sliced thin

½ red bell pepper, cut into strips

½ green bell pepper, cut into strips

1 tsp. coconut oil or olive oil

1 tsp. vegan butter

1 (14–16 oz.) package firm tofu,
drained and crumbled

Salt to taste

Pepper to taste

½ cup diced tomatoes

1 (15-oz.) can black soybeans, drained
and rinsed

Optional toppings/extras:

2–4 Tbsp. Daiya brand shredded cheese
of your choice

1–2 tsp. nutritional yeast

1 cup cauliflower rice

Chopped green onions

Fresh cilantro or parsley, chopped

1. Cook the onion and bell peppers in the coconut oil; remove from pan and cover to keep warm.

2. Melt the vegan butter in the pan and add in the crumbled tofu, salt, and pepper, and cook until warmed through. Remove from the pan; cover to keep warm.

3. Add the tomatoes and black soybeans to the pan and heat thoroughly.

4. Assemble your breakfast bowls with all of the above ingredients and optional toppings you desire.

Serving suggestion:

You can omit the tofu and sauté portobello mushrooms and spinach for additional toppings.

TIP
This would also be a great lunch or dinner.

Calories 231
Fat 12
Sodium 96
Carbs 14
Sugar 3
Protein 19

Soups & Chilies

Onion Soup

Lucille Amos
Greensboro, NC

Makes 10 servings
Prep. Time: 30 minutes ⚭ *Cooking Time: 4–5 hours* ⚭ *Ideal slow-cooker size: 4- to 5-qt.*

6 large onions
8 Tbsp. vegan butter
8 cups vegan vegetable broth
1 ½ tsp. coconut aminos
Pepper to taste
Vegan shredded mozzarella cheese

1. In large skillet or saucepan, sauté onions in butter until tender. Do not brown. Transfer to slow cooker.

2. Add vegetable broth, coconut aminos, and pepper.

3. Cover. Cook on Low 4–5 hours or until onions are very tender.

4. Top each serving with vegan mozzarella cheese.

Calories 99
Fat 7
Sodium 619
Carbs 8
Sugar 4
Protein 1

Tomato Basil Soup

Janet Melvin
Cincinnati, OH

Makes 12 servings
Prep. Time: 15 minutes ❧ Cooking Time: 3½ hours ❧ Ideal slow-cooker size: 4-qt.

½ cup very finely diced onion

2 cloves garlic, minced

2 cups vegan vegetable stock

2 (28-oz.) cans crushed tomatoes

¼ cup chopped fresh basil, plus more for garnish

1 Tbsp. salt

½ tsp. pepper

1 cup coconut cream, room temperature

1. Combine onion, garlic, stock, tomatoes, basil, salt, and pepper in slow cooker.

2. Cover and cook on High for 3 hours. May puree soup at this point if you wish for a totally smooth soup.

3. Stir in coconut cream *very* slowly while whisking continuously, and cook an additional 30 minutes on Low.

4. Garnish each serving with a few ribbons of fresh basil.

Calories 110
Fat 7
Sodium 852
Carbs 10
Sugar 5
Protein 3

SLOW-COOKER

Taco Soup

Hope Comerford
Clinton Township, MI

Makes 4–6 servings
Prep. Time: 10 minutes ⚭ *Cooking Time: 6 hours* ⚭ *Ideal slow-cooker size: 4-qt.*

2 lb. tofu crumbles

1 large onion, chopped

2 tsp. chili powder

2 tsp. garlic powder

1 tsp. dried parsley

1 tsp. onion powder

½ tsp. ground cumin

½ tsp. paprika

½ tsp. dried dill

2 tsp. sea salt

½ tsp. dried oregano

¼ tsp. black pepper

⅛ tsp. cayenne pepper

2 (14½-oz.) cans diced tomatoes

4 cups vegan vegetable broth

1. Place all ingredients into the crock and stir.

2. Cover and cook on Low for 6 hours.

Serving suggestion:

Serve with vegan shredded cheese and chunks of avocado.

Calories 186
Fat 7
Sodium 1132
Carbs 15
Sugar 3
Protein 15

Tofutilla Soup

Hope Comerford
Clinton Township, MI

Makes 6–8 servings
Prep. Time: 10 minutes   ⚕   Cooking Time: 6 hours   ⚕   Ideal slow-cooker size: 5-qt.

3 large tomatoes, chopped

1 cup chopped red onion

1 jalapeño, seeded and minced

2 tsp. cumin

2 tsp. chili powder

2 tsp. onion powder

2 tsp. garlic powder

2 tsp. lime juice

8 cups vegan vegetable broth

2 (8-oz.) blocks tempeh, cut into thin strips

Optional garnish:

Fresh chopped cilantro

Avocado slices

Vegan mozzarella cheese

1. In your crock, place the tomatoes, onion, and jalapeño.

2. Add all the seasonings and lime juice and pour in the vegetable broth.

3. Place the tempeh strips on top.

4. Cover and cook on Low for 6 hours.

5. If desired, serve each bowl of soup with fresh chopped cilantro, avocado slices, and freshly grated vegan mozzarella cheese.

TIP

If you don't have time for freshly chopped tomatoes, use a can of diced or chopped tomatoes.

Calories 152

Fat 6

Sodium 340

Carbs 14

Sugar 3

Protein 12

Italian Soup

Wendy B. Martzall
New Holland, PA

Makes 8 servings
Prep. Time: 15–20 minutes ⚬ Cooking Time: 5 hours 15 minutes ⚬ Ideal slow-cooker size: 3- to 4-qt.

1 lb. tofu crumbles
1 medium onion, chopped
1 small green bell pepper, chopped
1 (28-oz.) can diced tomatoes
4 cups vegetable broth
1 (8-oz.) can no-salt-added tomato sauce
2 tsp. Frank's RedHot Sauce
2 tsp. coconut aminos
7 drops liquid stevia
1 tsp. dried basil
½ tsp. dried oregano
1 (10-oz.) package frozen spinach, thawed and squeezed dry
½ cup nutritional yeast flakes

1. Add all ingredients except spinach and yeast to the crock. Stir until well blended.

2. Cover. Cook on Low 5 hours.

3. Stir spinach into soup. Cover and continue cooking on Low another 15 minutes.

4. Top each individual serving with a sprinkling of the nutritional yeast flakes.

Calories 121
Fat 3
Sodium 596
Carbs 14
Sugar 3
Protein 9

Cabbage Soup

Margaret Jarrett
Anderson, IN

Makes 8 servings
Prep. Time: 25 minutes ☙ Cooking Time: 6–7 hours ☙ Ideal slow-cooker size: 4-qt.

½ head of cabbage, sliced thin

2 ribs celery, sliced thin

½ cup chopped cauliflower

¼ cup chopped celery

1 (14-oz.) can diced tomatoes

1 onion, chopped

2 cups vegetable broth

2 cloves garlic, minced

1 qt. unsalted tomato juice (make sure it has no added sugar)

¼ tsp. pepper

Water

1. Combine all ingredients except water in slow cooker. Add water to within 3 inches of top of slow cooker.

2. Cover. Cook on Low 6–7 hours, or until vegetables are tender.

Calories 53
Fat 1
Sodium 498
Carbs 9
Sugar 5
Protein 3

Meatless Sausage and Cabbage Soup

Donna Suter
Pandora, OH

Makes 6–8 servings
Prep. Time: 10 minutes ☙ Cooking Time: 6 hours ☙ Ideal slow-cooker size: 4-qt.

16 oz. tofu crumbles
6 cups vegetable broth
1 onion, chopped
½ head cabbage, chopped
4–6 ribs celery, sliced
1 (14-oz.) can diced tomatoes
4 cloves garlic, chopped
2 tsp. coconut aminos
2 tsp. dried basil
1 tsp. salt
½ tsp. pepper

1. Add all ingredients to the slow cooker.

2. Cover and cook on Low for 6 hours.

Calories 80
Fat 3
Sodium 954
Carbs 8
Sugar 2
Protein 6

Cabbage Crumble Soup

Colleen Heatwole
Burton, MI

Makes 6–8 servings
Prep. Time: 20 minutes ⚜ Cooking Time: 6–8 hours ⚜ Ideal slow-cooker size: 5-qt.

I lb. tofu crumbles

I (28-oz. or 32-oz.) can diced tomatoes

½ tsp. garlic salt

¼ tsp. onion powder

¼ tsp. garlic powder

¼ tsp. pepper

2 ribs celery, chopped

½ medium head cabbage, chopped

2 tsp. coconut aminos

4 cups vegetable broth

Chopped fresh parsley, for garnish

1. Add all ingredients, except parsley, to the crock.

2. Cover and cook 6–8 hours on Low.

3. Serve in bowls garnished with fresh parsley.

Calories 86
Fat 3
Sodium 429
Carbs 10
Sugar 2
Protein 5

Stuffed Pepper Soup

SLOW-COOKER

Shelia Heil
Lancaster, PA

Makes 8–10 servings
Prep. Time: 45 minutes ⚓ Cooking Time:4–5 hours ⚓ Ideal slow-cooker size: 6-qt.

1 lb. tofu crumbles

1 small onion, diced

1 large green bell pepper, diced

1 large red bell pepper, diced

1 (26-oz.) can diced tomatoes

1 (8-oz.) can tomato sauce

2 cups vegan vegetable broth

15 drops liquid stevia

2 tsp. coconut aminos

1 tsp. garlic powder

Salt to taste

Pepper to taste

1. Add all ingredients to the crock and stir.

2. Cover and cook on Low 4–5 hours, to meld flavors.

Calories 71
Fat 8
Sodium 352
Carbs 8
Sugar 2
Protein 5

Zucchini Stew

Colleen Heatwole
Burton, MI

Makes 6 servings
Prep. Time: 30 minutes   ✤   *Cooking Time: 4–6 hours*   ✤   *Ideal slow-cooker size: 6-qt.*

1 lb. meatless sausage crumbles

2 ribs of celery, diced

2 (28-oz.) cans of diced tomatoes

4 cups vegetable broth

2 lb. zucchini, cut into ½-inch slices

2 medium green bell peppers, diced

1 medium onion, chopped

2 cloves garlic, minced

5 drops liquid stevia

1 tsp. oregano

1 tsp. Italian seasoning

1 tsp. salt, *optional* (taste first)

6 Tbsp. vegan Parmesan cheese or nutritional yeast flakes

1. Combine all ingredients, except vegan Parmesan cheese or nutritional yeast flakes, in the slow cooker.

2. Cook on Low 4–6 hours. Garnish each serving with 1 Tbsp. vegan Parmesan cheese or nutritional yeast flakes.

Calories 212
Fat 2
Sodium 962
Carbs 32
Sugar 9
Protein 14

Tempeh and Zucchini Stew

Jeanne Allen
Rye, CO

Makes 4–6 servings
Prep. Time: 20 minutes ☙ Cooking Time: 6 hours ☙ Ideal slow-cooker size: 4-qt.

2 lb. tempeh, cubed

1 large onion, diced

2 cloves garlic, minced

2 Tbsp. olive oil

3 cups vegetable broth

2 tsp. coconut aminos

1 Tbsp. dried parsley flakes

1 tsp. ground cumin

½ tsp. salt

3 zucchini, diced

1 (14½-oz.) can diced tomatoes

1 (14½-oz.) can green beans, drained,
or 1 lb. frozen green beans

1 (4-oz.) can diced green chilies

1. Stir together all ingredients in the crock.

2. Cover. Cook on Low for 6 hours.

Calories 261
Fat 13
Sodium 525
Carbs 22
Sugar 7
Protein 18

Tempeh Vegetable Soup

Hope Comerford
Clinton Township, MI

Makes 6 servings
Prep. Time: 20 minutes ⚭ Cooking Time: 6 hours ⚭ Ideal slow-cooker size: 4-qt.

2 lb. tempeh, cut into 1-inch chunks
1 large red onion, chopped
2 cups vegetable broth
1 (6-oz.) can tomato paste
2 tsp. coconut aminos
4 cloves garlic, minced
1 Tbsp. paprika
2 tsp. dried marjoram
½ tsp. black pepper
1 tsp. sea salt
1 red bell pepper, sliced
1 yellow bell pepper, sliced
1 orange bell pepper, sliced

1. Place all ingredients in the crock except the sliced bell peppers, and stir.

2. Cover and cook on Low for 6 hours. Stir in sliced bell peppers the last 45 minutes of cooking time.

Calories 349
Fat 17
Sodium 424
Carbs 26
Sugar 6
Protein 33

Mixed Vegetable Tempeh Soup

Grace Ketcham
Marietta, GA

SLOW-COOKER

Makes 4–6 servings
Prep. Time: 15 minutes ⚹ Cooking Time: 7 hours ⚹ Ideal slow-cooker size: 4½-qt.

2 lb. tempeh, cubed
1 (8-oz.) can tomato sauce
1 tsp. coconut aminos
1 garlic clove, minced
1 medium onion, chopped
2 bay leaves
½ tsp. salt
½ tsp. paprika
¼ tsp. pepper
Dash ground cloves or allspice
1 (14-oz.) can diced tomatoes
1 cup chopped green beans
2 cups chopped cauliflower
2 ribs celery, chopped
½ cup water

1. Combine all ingredients in slow cooker.

2. Cover. Cook on Low 7 hours. Remove bay leaves and serve.

Calories 346
Fat 17
Sodium 534
Carbs 23
Sugar 5
Protein 33

SLOW-COOKER

Meatless Meatball Stew

Barbara Hershey
Lititz, PA

Makes 8 servings
Prep. Time: 15 minutes ⚘ *Cooking Time: 6–7 hours* ⚘ *Ideal slow-cooker size: 4- or 6-qt.*

2 lb. meatless meatballs
4 cups chopped cauliflower
1 large onion, sliced
2 cups chopped broccoli
4 cups no-sugar-added tomato juice
1 tsp. dried basil
1 tsp. dried oregano
½ tsp. pepper
Salt to taste

1. Place all ingredients in the slow cooker.

2. Cover. Cook on Low 6–7 hours, or until vegetables are tender.

Calories 123
Fat 4
Sodium 529
Carbs 13
Sugar 6
Protein 11

Seasoned Chili

Sharon Miller
Holmesville, OH

Makes 6 servings
Prep. Time: 15 minutes ⚭ *Cooking Time: 5–6 hours* ⚭ *Ideal slow-cooker size: 4-qt.*

2 lb. tofu crumbles

2 (14-oz.) cans diced tomatoes, undrained, *divided*

2 Tbsp. vegan butter

1 cup diced onion

1 cup diced red bell pepper

1–2 Tbsp. chili powder, according to your taste preference

1 tsp. ground cumin

1 tsp. ground oregano

Salt to taste

Pepper to taste

1. Add all the ingredients to the slow cooker.

2. Cover and cook on Low for 5–6 hours.

Serving suggestion:

Can be served with vegan shredded cheddar cheese, vegan sour cream, and avocado slices.

Calories 201
Fat 10
Sodium 262
Carbs 14
Sugar 3
Protein 14

Vegan Chili

Jewel Showalter
Landisville, PA

Makes 6–8 servings
Prep. Time: 10 minutes ⚜ *Cooking Time: 6 hours* ⚜ *Ideal slow-cooker size: 5-qt.*

16 oz. tofu crumbles

1 (15½-oz.) can black soybeans, rinsed, drained

2 chopped onions

2 cloves garlic, minced

2–4 (4¼-oz.) cans chopped green chilies, drained, depending on your taste preference

1–2 diced jalapeño peppers

2 tsp. ground cumin

1½ tsp. dried oregano

¼ tsp. cayenne pepper

½ tsp. salt

6 cups water

Optional:

1–2 cups shredded vegan cheese

Vegan sour cream

Salsa

Avocado chunks

1. Place all ingredients except the optional toppings into the crock.

2. Cover. Cook on Low 6 hours.

3. Serve topped with optional toppings if desired.

Calories 131
Fat 5
Sodium 150
Carbs 12
Sugar 4
Protein 11

Spicy Hot Beefless Chili

Maria Shevlin
Sicklerville, NJ

Makes 6–8 servings

Prep. Time: 30 minutes ☙ Cooking Time: 3 hours ☙ Ideal slow-cooker size: 6-qt.

1 large onion, diced

3 cloves garlic, minced

1 small red bell pepper, diced fine

1 (14½-oz.) can petite diced tomatoes (do not drain)

1–1½ cups vegetable stock, depend on how thick you like your chili

1 (15½-oz.) can black soybeans, rinsed, drained

¼ cup tomato paste

1½ tsp. chili powder

1 tsp. cumin

1 tsp. smoked paprika

1 tsp. garlic powder

1 tsp. salt

½–1 tsp. cayenne pepper

½ tsp. black pepper

Pinch red pepper flakes

1 (13.7-oz.) bag Gardein Beefless Ground

1. Add all ingredients except the Gardein Beefless Ground to the crock and stir.

2. Cover and cook on Low for 3 hours.

3. Stir well and add the beefless crumbles and mix once again.

4. Cover and cook for an additional 3–5 minutes only.

5. Serve immediately.

Serving Suggestion:

Serve with Daiya brand cheese and a homemade vegan sour cream if desired. Top with green onion and additional hot sauce if you really want to kick it up even more. You can serve this with shirataki rice or atop shirataki noodles for a Cincinnati-type chili.

TIP

The brand of meatless crumbles I used suggests no long cooking time. They can be added at the last 3–5 minutes of the cooking time. Also, note you can also make this without the brand of crumbles I used, and instead use a block of tofu, crumbled.

Calories 127

Fat 5

Sodium 420

Carbs 13

Sugar 3

Protein 10

Tempeh Chili

Carol Duree
Salina, KS

Makes 5 servings
Prep. Time: 15 minutes ⚸ *Cooking Time: 5 hours* ⚸ *Ideal slow-cooker size: 4-qt.*

1 lb. tempeh, sliced or cut into 1-inch chunks

2 (14½-oz.) cans diced tomatoes

1 (4¼-oz.) can diced green chili peppers, drained

½ cup chopped onion

1 clove garlic, minced

1 Tbsp. chili powder

1. Layer ingredients into slow cooker in order given.

2. Cover. Cook on Low for 5 hours.

Calories 236
Fat 10
Sodium 324
Carbs 20
Sugar 3
Protein 20

Hearty Chili

Ruth Shank
Gridley, IL

Makes 10–12 servings
Prep. Time: 20 minutes & Cooking Time: 4 hours & Ideal slow-cooker size: 5-qt.

2 lb. meatless crumbles

1 (15½-oz.) can black soybeans, drained and rinsed

¼ cup chopped onions

1 rib celery, chopped

1 Tbsp. olive oil

1 (29-oz.) can stewed tomatoes

½ cup tomato sauce

1½ tsp. lemon juice

2 tsp. white rice vinegar

¾ tsp. Truvia brown sugar blend

1½ tsp. salt

1 tsp. liquid aminos

½ tsp. garlic powder

½ tsp. dry mustard powder

1 Tbsp. chili powder

2 (6-oz.) cans tomato paste

1. Place all ingredients into slow cooker. Mix well.

2. Cover. Cook on Low for 5 hours.

Serving Suggestion:

Top with diced avocado and sprinkled with vegan shredded cheese.

Calories 189
Fat 9
Sodium 912
Carbs 20
Sugar 6
Protein 12

Hearty Vegan Chili

Joylynn Keener
Lancaster, PA

Makes 8 servings
Prep. Time: 20–25 minutes ⚜ *Cooking Time: 5–6 hours* ⚜ *Ideal slow-cooker size: 5-qt.*

32 oz. meatless crumbles

1 (15½-oz.) can black soybeans, drained, rinsed

1 onion, chopped

2 ribs celery, chopped

1 Tbsp. olive oil

1 (14-oz.) can diced tomatoes

2 (14-oz.) cans tomato sauce

1 green bell pepper, chopped

15 drops liquid stevia

1 tsp. salt

1 tsp. dried thyme

1 tsp. dried oregano

1 Tbsp. chili powder, or to taste

1. Place all ingredients into slow cooker, mixing well.

2. Cover. Cook on Low 5–6 hours.

Calories 154
Fat 7
Sodium 823
Carbs 12
Sugar 5
Protein 11

Texican Tempeh Chili

Becky Oswald
Broadway, VA

Makes 15 servings
Prep. Time: 20 minutes ⚘ Cooking Time: 6 hours ⚘ Ideal slow-cooker size: 5- to 6-qt.

8 vegan bacon strips, diced

2 Tbsp. avocado oil, *divided*

2½ lb. tempeh, cubed

1 (28-oz.) can stewed tomatoes

1 (14½-oz.) can stewed tomatoes

2 (8-oz.) cans tomato sauce

1 medium onion, chopped

1 cup chopped celery

2 cups chopped bell pepper (any color(s))

¼ cup minced fresh parsley

1 Tbsp. chili powder

1 tsp. salt

½ tsp. ground cumin

¼ tsp. pepper

1. Cook bacon in skillet with 1 Tbsp. avocado oil until crisp. Pour into crock.

2. Brown tempeh cubes in skillet with the other 1 Tbsp. avocado oil. Pour into crock.

3. Place all the remaining ingredients in the slow cooker and stir to combine.

4. Cover. Cook on Low 6 hours.

Calories 196
Fat 11
Sodium 487
Carbs 12
Sugar 4
Protein 17

Chili Con No Carne

Donna Conto
Saylorsburg, PA

Makes 4–6 servings
Prep. Time: 15 minutes & Cooking Time: 5–6 hours & Ideal slow-cooker size: 4-qt.

1½ lb. meatless crumbles
1 cup chopped onions
¾ cup chopped green peppers
1 garlic clove, minced
1 (14½-oz.) can chopped tomatoes
1 (8-oz.) can tomato sauce
2 tsp. chili powder
½ tsp. dried basil

1. Combine all ingredients in slow cooker.

2. Cover. Cook on Low 5–6 hours.

Calories 132
Fat 6
Sodium 311
Carbs 11
Sugar 5
Protein 11

Main Dishes

Blueberry & Tofu Salad

Mary Fisher
Leola, PA

Makes 4 main-dish servings
Prep. Time: 30 minutes ⚜ Chilling Time: 30 minutes or more

I Tbsp. coconut oil

I lb. extra-firm tofu, cubed

¾ cup chopped celery

½ cup diced sweet red pepper

½ cup thinly sliced green onions

2 cups fresh blueberries

6-oz. nondairy plain yogurt

I tsp. stevia granules

3 Tbsp. Vegenaise Dressing and Sandwich Spread

½ tsp. sea salt

4 cups chopped Bibb lettuce

1. Heat coconut oil in a skillet and brown tofu cubes.

2. In a large bowl, gently combine the browned tofu cubes, celery, red pepper, onions, and blueberries.

3. In a separate bowl, combine yogurt, stevia, Vegenaise, and salt.

4. Drizzle dressing mixture over tofu cubes and gently toss to coat.

5. Cover and refrigerate at least 30 minutes.

6. Divide the lettuce among 4 plates and evenly divide the tofu mixture over the top of each.

Serving suggestion:

Garnish with fresh chopped mint.

Calories 253
Fat 14
Sodium 312
Carbs 23
Sugar 13
Protein 13

Zesty Black Bean & Tofu Salad

CHILLED

Hope Comerford
Clinton Township, MI

Makes 4 servings
Prep. Time: 15 minutes ⚭ Marinating Time: 2 hours

2 (15½-oz.) cans black soybeans, drained and rinsed

1 lb. extra-firm tofu, crumbled

1½ tomatoes, chopped

1 cup chopped red sweet bell pepper

¾ cup chopped red onion

4–6 cloves minced garlic, according to your taste preference

½ cup chopped fresh cilantro

1 minced jalapeño, or 1 (4-oz.) can chopped green chilies

⅓ cup olive oil

½ cup lemon juice

¼ tsp. white pepper

4 cups chopped mixed greens

1. Mix all ingredients except mixed greens in a large bowl.

2. Let marinate in the refrigerator for 2 hours.

3. Evenly divide the mixed greens among 4 plates and serve the bean salad divided evenly atop the 4 plates of mixed greens.

Serving suggestion:

Sprinkle with nutritional yeast flakes if desired.

Calories 592
Fat 24
Sodium 30
Carbs 65
Sugar 5
Protein 32

Main Dishes 🌿 79

Italian Bean Salad

CHILLED

Kathy Stoltzfus
Leola, PA

Makes 4 servings
Prep. Time: 20 minutes ⚜ Cooking Time: 15 minutes ⚜ Marinating Time: 45 minutes

2 Tbsp. olive oil

2 Tbsp. vegan balsamic vinegar

Black pepper

1 lb. cooked cauliflower rice

2 (15½-oz.) cans black soybeans, rinsed and drained

½ large cucumber, peeled, halved lengthwise and thinly sliced

3 green onions, chopped

1 large sweet bell pepper, chopped

¼ cup fresh basil, chopped

¼ cup fresh parsley, chopped

Lettuce leaves

1 large tomato, cut into wedges

1. In a large bowl, whisk together oil, vinegar, and black pepper.

2. Add cauliflower rice, beans, cucumber, onions, bell pepper, basil, and parsley to the oil and vinegar mixture. Toss well.

3. Cover and marinate in the regrigerator for 45 minutes.

4. Serve on lettuce with tomato wedges.

Calories 325
Fat 17
Sodium 95
Carbs 27
Sugar 9
Protein 22

Beans with Peppers and Tomatoes

STOVETOP

Rika Allen
New Holland, PA

Makes 2 main-dish servings
Prep. Time: 15 minutes ⚭ Cooking Time: 25–30 minutes

I Tbsp. olive oil

½ cup chopped onion

2 tsp. garlic, minced

I tsp. ground turmeric

I tsp. ground cumin

I tsp. ground coriander

2 cups (I large) diced bell sweet pepper, your choice of colors

I cup (I medium) diced tomatoes

I (15½-oz.) can black soybeans, rinsed and drained

2 Tbsp. water

Dash pepper

1. In a good-sized skillet or saucepan, heat olive oil and sauté onion and garlic until translucent.

2. Stir in turmeric, cumin, and coriander.

3. Add pepper and tomato and sauté.

4. Then add the black soybeans.

5. Stir in water. Cover. Reduce heat and cook for about 15 minutes, or until vegetables are cooked to your liking.

6. Add pepper and cook another minute.

Serving suggestion:

Serve as is, or over cooked cauliflower rice.

Calories 349
Fat 17
Sodium 256
Carbs 32
Sugar 8
Protein 21

Spinach-Stuffed Tomatoes

Hope Comerford
Clinton Township, MI

Makes 4 servings
Prep. Time: 15–20 minutes ⚭ Cooking/Baking Time: 35 minutes

OVEN

8 medium tomatoes
1 ½ lb. fresh spinach
2 Tbsp. finely chopped onion
2 Tbsp. coconut oil
½ cup full-fat coconut cream
½ cup soft tofu
½ tsp. salt
⅛ tsp. pepper
1 cup shredded vegan cheese

1. Slice off top of each tomato and scoop out the pulp and seeds.

2. Place the spinach and onion in saucepan with coconut oil. Cook over medium heat until onions are softened and spinach is completely wilted down.

3. In a small bowl, combine coconut cream, soft tofu, salt, and pepper.

4. Stir into spinach and onions. Cook for an additional minute.

5. Spoon the spinach mixture into the tomatoes evenly.

6. Place the tomatoes in a lightly greased baking dish.

7. Bake, uncovered, at 350°F for 25 minutes.

8. The last 5 minutes of cooking time, top each tomato with the shredded vegan cheese.

Calories 355
Fat 25
Sodium 641
Carbs 26
Sugar 7
Protein 11

Stuffed Peppers

Angela Newcomer Buller
Beavercreek, OH

Makes 4–6 servings
Prep. Time: 30 minutes & Cooking/Baking Time: 45–50 minutes

4–5 green bell peppers

1 (15½-oz.) can black soybeans, drained and rinsed

2 cups cooked cauliflower rice

1 cup vegan shredded cheddar cheese

1 Tbsp. chili powder

Pinch ground cumin

1 (24-oz.) can tomato sauce

2 cloves garlic, minced

1 tsp. dried oregano

1 tsp. dried basil

1. Cut tops off peppers and remove seeds and white ribs.

2. In a bowl, combine soybeans, cauliflower rice, vegan shredded cheddar cheese, chili powder, and cumin.

3. Spoon the mixture evenly into the peppers, pushing gently if needed.

4. Place peppers in a casserole dish. Cover.

5. Bake at 350°F for 45–50 minutes.

6. While the peppers are baking, pour tomato sauce in saucepan and add the garlic, oregano, and basil.

7. Heat on low until hot. Serve sauce with peppers.

TIP

For a lovely presentation, cut the peppers in half on the plate and spoon the tomato sauce over top.

Calories 68

Fat 3

Sodium 369

Carbs 5

Sugar 1

Protein 8

Vegan Stuffed Cabbage

Becky Gehman
Bergton, VA

Makes 6 servings
Prep. Time: 15–20 minutes   Cooking Time: 1 hour, 40 minutes

6–7 large cabbage leaves
1 lb. meatless crumbles
1 tsp. finely diced onion
¼ tsp. salt
½ tsp. pepper
3 Tbsp. cauliflower rice, uncooked
1⅓ cups tomato sauce
10 oz. water
1 tsp. Italian seasoning
1 Tbsp. white rice vinegar

Serving suggestion:
Sprinkle with nutritional yeast.

1. Place cabbage leaves in large stockpot. Cover with water. Cover pot and cook cabbage until just tender. Remove leaves from water and drain.

2. Mix meatless crumbles, onion, salt, pepper, and cauliflower rice together in a bowl.

3. Divide this mixture among the 6 or 7 cooked cabbage leaves. Place in the middle of each leaf.

4. Wrap cabbage leaves around meat mixture to make bundles. Secure each with 2 toothpicks to keep them from unwrapping.

5. Heat tomato sauce, water, and Italian seasoning if you wish, in a large saucepan.

6. Carefully lay cabbage bundles in tomato sauce mixture.

7. Allow to simmer, covered, 1½ hours.

8. Stir in vinegar 10 minutes before end of cooking time.

Calories 81
Fat 4
Sodium 350
Carbs 6
Sugar 3
Protein 7

Zucchini Crumble Casserole

Judi Manos
West Islip, NY

Makes 6 servings
Prep. Time: 20 minutes ⚭ Cooking/Baking Time: 50–65 minutes

2 tsp. olive oil

½ cup finely chopped onions

I lb. (3 small) zucchini, cut into ¼-inch-thick slices

¼ lb. fresh mushrooms, sliced

I lb. meatless crumbles

I (14½-oz.) can sliced tomatoes, undrained, no salt added

½ tsp. garlic powder

½ tsp. dried oregano

¼ cup nutritional yeast flakes

1. Preheat oven to 350°F.

2. Heat oil in large skillet. Add onions and stir until tender and light golden in color.

3. Add zucchini and mushrooms to skillet. Cook over medium heat 3–4 minutes, stirring lightly.

4. Put zucchini mixture into lightly greased 2-qt. baking dish.

5. Place meatless crumbles in skillet. Cook over medium heat, stirring frequently.

6. Add tomatoes, garlic powder, and oregano to skillet. Mix well.

7. Spoon mixture over zucchini in baking dish.

8. Sprinkle nutritional yeast on top.

9. Bake, uncovered, 35–45 minutes, or until cheese is lightly browned and dish is heated through.

Calories 165
Fat 6
Sodium 332
Carbs 17
Sugar 4
Protein 11

OVEN

Mushroom Risotto

Hope Comerford
Clinton Township, MI

Makes 4 main-dish servings
Prep. Time: 15 minutes ⁂ Cooking Time: 20–25 minutes ⁂ Standing Time: 5 minutes

2 Tbsp. extra-virgin olive oil, *divided*

½ cup finely chopped onion

2 cups chopped mushrooms

1 clove garlic minced

4 cups riced cauliflower

¼ cup vegetable broth

¼ cup nutritional yeast flakes

½ tsp. salt

Freshly ground black pepper, *optional*

1. Heat 1 Tbsp. olive oil in a large skillet. Add chopped onion, mushrooms, and garlic and stir to coat with olive oil. Cook until onions are softened.

2. Add additional Tbsp. of olive oil and riced cauliflower and stir to coat well. Cook 4–5 more minutes, stirring frequently.

3. Pour in vegetable broth, nutritional yeast, salt, and pepper (if using). Stir. Continue cooking until all broth has evaporated.

Calories 118
Fat 7
Sodium 298
Carbs 10
Sugar 3
Protein 5

Open-Face Portobello Mushroom Sandwiches

OVEN

Hope Comerford
Clinton Township, MI

Makes 4 servings
Prep. Time: 15 minutes & Marinating Time: 1 hour & Cooking Time: 10 minutes

4 large portobello mushrooms, stems removed

¼ cup vegan balsamic vinegar

¼ cup olive oil

¼ tsp. salt

¼ tsp. freshly ground pepper

8 oz. GoVeggie Chive & Garlic Cream Cheese Alternative

4 tomato slices

4 red onion slices

I cup microgreens

1. Place mushrooms in a large resealable bag with the balsamic vinegar and olive oil. Seal the bag.

2. Toss to coat, and then marinate for 1 hour.

3. Preheat oven to 350°F.

4. Remove mushrooms from the marinade. Season both sides with salt and pepper.

5. Place mushrooms on a greased cookie sheet and spread the GoVeggie Chive & Garlic Cream Cheese Alternative evenly among the inside cavity of the mushrooms.

6. Bake uncovered for 18–20 minutes.

7. Remove from oven and place a slice of tomato and onion on each mushroom. Evenly distribute the microgreens between each mushroom. Serve immediately.

Calories 397
Fat 33
Sodium 309
Carbs 21
Sugar 11
Protein 6

Tofu Lettuce Wraps

Hope Comerford
Clinton Township, MI

Makes About 12 wraps
Prep. Time: 15 minutes ⚜ Cooking Time: 2¼–3¼ hours ⚜ Ideal slow-cooker size: 5- or 7-qt.

2 lb. meatless crumbles

4 cloves garlic, minced

½ cup minced sweet yellow onion

4 Tbsp. coconut aminos

1 Tbsp. natural crunchy no-sugar-added peanut butter

1 tsp. white rice vinegar

1 tsp. sesame oil

¼ tsp. kosher salt

¼ tsp. red pepper flakes

¼ tsp. black pepper

3 green onions, sliced

1 (8-oz.) can sliced water chestnuts, drained, rinsed, chopped

12 good-sized pieces of iceberg lettuce, rinsed and patted dry

1. In the crock, combine the meatless crumbles, garlic, yellow onion, coconut aminos, peanut butter, vinegar, sesame oil, salt, red pepper flakes, and black pepper.

2. Cover and cook on Low for 2–3 hours.

3. Add in the green onions and water chestnuts. Cover and cook for an additional 10–15 minutes.

4. Serve a good spoonful on each piece of iceberg lettuce.

Serving Suggestion:

Garnish with diced red bell pepper and diced green onion.

Calories 98
Fat 5
Sodium 276
Carbs 8
Sugar 2
Protein 8

Caponata & Tofu Dinner

Katrine Rose
Woodbridge, VA

Makes 4–6 servings
Prep. Time: 20 minutes ⚘ *Cooking Time: 7–8 hours* ⚘ *Ideal slow-cooker size: 4-qt.*

1 medium (1 lb.) eggplant, peeled and cut into ½-inch cubes

16 oz. tofu crumbles

1 (14-oz.) can diced tomatoes

1 medium onion, chopped

1 red bell pepper, cut into ½-inch pieces

¾ cup fresh salsa

¼ cup olive oil

2 Tbsp. capers, drained

3 Tbsp. vegan balsamic vinegar

3 cloves garlic, minced

1¼ tsp. dried oregano

⅓ cup, packed, chopped fresh basil

1. Combine all ingredients except basil in slow cooker.

2. Cover. Cook on Low 7–8 hours, or until vegetables are tender.

3. Stir in basil.

Serving suggestion:

Serve in keto/vegan-friendly wraps.

Calories 204
Fat 13
Sodium 416
Carbs 15
Sugar 7
Protein 8

Sautéed Tofu with Spinach

STOVETOP

Donna Treloar
Muncie, IN

Makes 2 servings
Prep. Time: 5 minutes & Cooking Time: 5 minutes

6 oz. firm fresh tofu

2 Tbsp. extra-virgin olive oil

1 clove garlic, minced

8 oz. fresh spinach, washed

2 Tbsp. vegan balsamic vinegar

1. Cut tofu in thin strips.

2. Heat oil in large saucepan.

3. Sauté tofu strips until brown on one side.

4. Stir in garlic and turn the tofu strips as you do so.

5. Toss in spinach and vinegar. Cover saucepan.

6. Cook for 1 minute or until spinach wilts.

7. Remove from heat and serve.

TIP

I like to spray this dish with liquid aminos seasoning just before serving.

Calories 227
Fat 17
Sodium 110
Carbs 10
Sugar 3
Protein 11

Garlic and Lemon Tofu

Hope Comerford
Clinton Township, MI

Makes 4 servings
Prep. Time: 10 minutes plus pressing time ⚜ *Cooking Time: 4–5 hours* ⚜ *Ideal slow-cooker size: 3-qt.*

2 (14-oz.) packages extra-firm tofu, pressed, and cut into 1-inch chunks

½ cup minced shallots

½ cup olive oil

¼ cup lemon juice

3 medium cloves garlic, minced

1 Tbsp. no-salt seasoning

⅛ tsp. pepper

1. Place tofu in slow cooker.

2. In a small bowl, mix the remaining ingredients. Pour this mixture over the tofu in the crock.

3. Cover and cook on Low for 4–5 hours.

Calories 421
Fat 35
Sodium 26
Carbs 9
Sugar 2
Protein 19

Tofu Cacciatore

SLOW-COOKER

Ann Driscoll
Albuquerque, NM

Makes 4–6 servings
Prep. Time: 10 minutes plus pressing time ⚘ Cooking Time: 4 hours ⚘ Ideal slow-cooker size: 4-qt.

1 large onion, thinly sliced

2 (14-oz.) packages extra-firm tofu, pressed and cut into 1-inch chunks

2 (6-oz.) cans tomato paste

4 oz. sliced mushrooms

1 tsp. sea salt

¼ cup vegan vegetable broth

¼ tsp. pepper

1–2 cloves garlic, minced

1–2 tsp. dried oregano

½ tsp. dried basil

½ tsp. celery seed, *optional*

1 bay leaf

1. Place onion in slow cooker. Add tofu chunks.

2. Combine remaining ingredients. Pour over tofu.

3. Cover. Cook on Low 4 hours.

Serving suggestion:

Serve over shirataki noodles and sprinkle with nutritional yeast flakes.

Calories 173
Fat 6
Sodium 881
Carbs 17
Sugar 8
Protein 16

Tempeh Cacciatore

Darla Sathre
Baxter, MN

Makes 4 servings
Prep. Time: 5–10 minutes ⚜ Cooking Time: 5 hours ⚜ Ideal slow-cooker size: 4-qt.

16 oz. tempeh
2 onions, thinly sliced
3 cloves garlic, minced
¼ tsp. pepper
2 tsp. dried oregano
1 tsp. dried basil
1 bay leaf
2 (15-oz.) cans diced tomatoes
1 (8-oz.) can tomato sauce
1 (4-oz.) can sliced mushrooms

1. Slice each block of tempeh into two pieces, so you'll have 4 squares.

2. Place onions in bottom of slow cooker. Add tempeh on top and the remaining ingredients.

3. Cover. Cook on Low 5 hours.

Serving suggestion:

Serve over shirataki noodles and sprinkle with nutritional yeast flakes.

Calories 223
Fat 9
Sodium 514
Carbs 22
Sugar 5
Protein 18

Tofu Dijon Dinner

Barbara Stutzman
Crossville, TN

SLOW-COOKER

Makes 4–6 servings

Prep. Time: 20 minutes plus pressing time ⚭ *Cooking Time: 4 hours* ⚭ *Ideal slow-cooker size: 6-qt.*

14 oz. extra-firm tofu, pressed and cut into 1-inch chunks

2 cloves garlic, minced

1 Tbsp. olive oil

6 Tbsp. white rice vinegar

4 Tbsp. coconut aminos

4 Tbsp. Maille Dijon mustard

1 lb. sliced mushrooms

1. Grease interior of crock.

2. Place tofu chunks in crock.

3. Stir together garlic, oil, vinegar, coconut aminos, and mustard until well mixed.

4. Gently stir in mushrooms.

5. Spoon sauce into crock, and stir to coat all tofu.

6. Cover. Cook on Low for 4 hours.

7. Serve tofu topped with the sauce.

Serving suggestion:

Serve over cauliflower rice.

Calories 81
Fat 5
Sodium 680
Carbs 2
Sugar 0
Protein 7

Southwestern Tofu

Hope Comerford
Clinton Township, MI

Makes 4–6 servings
Prep. Time: 8–10 minutes plus pressing time ⚭ Cooking Time: 5–6 hours ⚭ Ideal slow-cooker size: 3-qt.

2 (14-oz.) packages extra-firm tofu, pressed and cut into 1-inch chunks

1 Tbsp. chili powder

2 tsp. garlic powder

1 tsp. cumin

1 tsp. onion powder

½ tsp. kosher salt

¼ tsp. pepper

1 medium onion, chopped

1 (14½-oz.) can diced tomatoes

1 (4-oz.) can diced green chilies

½ cup vegan sour cream

Optional toppings:

Lettuce

Vegan shredded cheese

Vegan sour cream

Fresh salsa

1. Place the tofu chunks in the slow cooker.

2. Mix together the chili powder, garlic powder, cumin, onion powder, kosher salt, and pepper. Sprinkle this over the tofu.

3. Sprinkle the onion over the top of the tofu and pour the cans of diced tomatoes and green chilies over the top.

4. Cover and cook on Low for 5–6 hours.

5. Remove the tofu from the crock, leaving the juices.

6. Slowly whisk in the vegan sour cream with the juices in the crock. Replace the tofu in the crock and stir to mix in the sauce.

Serving suggestion:

Serve topped with some shredded lettuce, shredded cheese, vegan sour cream, and fresh salsa.

Calories 175
Fat 9
Sodium 333
Carbs 11
Sugar 2
Protein 14

Tempeh Fajitas

Becky Frey
Lebanon, PA

STOVETOP

Makes 4–6 servings
Prep. Time: 20–30 minutes ⚬ Marinating Time: 15 minutes ⚬ Cooking Time: 6–8 minutes

¼ cup lime juice

3 Tbsp. olive oil

1–2 cloves garlic, minced

1 tsp. chili powder

½ tsp. ground cumin

2 (8-oz.) blocks of tempeh, cut into strips

1 large onion, sliced

½ green bell sweet pepper, slivered

½ red bell sweet pepper, slivered

8–12 vegan keto wraps, such as coconut wraps or raw kale wraps

½ cup fresh salsa

½ cup vegan sour cream

½ cup vegan shredded cheese

1. Combine first five ingredients in a large bowl.

2. Add tempeh slices. Stir until tempeh is well coated.

3. Marinate for 15 minutes.

4. Cook tempeh mixture in large hot nonstick skillet for 3 minutes.

5. Stir in onion and peppers. Cook 3–5 minutes, or until done to your liking.

6. Divide mixture evenly among tortillas.

7. Top each with a bit of fresh salsa, vegan sour cream, and vegan shredded cheese.

8. Roll up and serve.

Calories 306
Fat 16
Sodium 253
Carbs 26
Sugar 3
Protein 21

Simple Tofu

Rika Allen
New Holland, PA

Makes 2 main-dish servings
Prep. Time: 7–10 minutes ⚜ Standing Time, if needed: 20 minutes ⚜ Cooking Time: 12–15 minutes

1 (14-oz.) package firm, light tofu
2 tsp. minced garlic
1 Tbsp. olive oil
1 Tbsp. coconut aminos

1. Place tofu on a microwave-safe plate lined with paper towel. Heat tofu, uncovered, for 4 minutes. If microwave oven is not available, place block of tofu on a paper towel on a cutting board. Cover with a paper towel and put a few cans of food as weight on top. Allow to stand 20 minutes. Discard water and pat tofu with paper towel.

2. Slice tofu into ⅓-inch-thick slices, or about 10 slices.

3. In a large nonstick skillet over medium heat, sauté garlic in olive oil.

4. Place tofu in skillet and brown over medium-high heat.

5. Flip with a metal spatula and brown the other side.

6. Drizzle coconut aminos evenly over tofu. Cook 1–2 minutes.

7. Flip one more time and cook 1 more minute.

TIP
Browning tofu is the key to the flavor of this recipe, and a nonstick pan makes this an easy recipe. Slightly burnt dark edges are particularly tasty.

Calories 225
Fat 5
Sodium 355
Carbs 16
Sugar 0
Protein 17

Marinated Tempeh

SLOW-COOKER

Susan Nafziger
Canton, KS

Makes 6 servings

Prep. Time: 15 minutes & Cooking Time: 5 hours & Marinating Time: 2–3 hours &
Ideal slow-cooker size: oval 5-qt.

1 cup olive oil

1 cup coconut aminos

¼ cup white rice vinegar

½ cup chopped onions

⅛ tsp. garlic powder

¼ tsp. ground ginger

½ tsp. black pepper (coarsely ground is best)

½ tsp. dry mustard

3–4 (8-oz.) blocks tempeh

1. Mix the first 8 ingredients, either by whisking together in a bowl or whirring the mixture in a blender.

2. Place tempeh in a low baking or serving dish and pour marinade over top. Cover and refrigerate for 2–3 hours.

3. Grease interior of slow-cooker crock.

4. Place tempeh in the crock. Pour marinade over top.

5. Cover. Cook on Low 5 hours.

6. Cut into slices or chunks. Top with marinade and serve.

Serving suggestion:

This would be good served alongside the Roasted Broccoli on page 161 or the Colorful Oven-Roasted Vegetables on page 197.

Calories 545
Fat 48
Sodium 1779
Carbs 12
Sugar 1
Protein 28

Szechuan-Style Tofu and Broccoli

SLOW-COOKER

Jane Meiser
Harrisonburg, VA

Makes 4 servings

Prep. Time: 30 minutes plus pressing time ⚘ *Cooking Time: 1½–3 hours* ⚘ *Ideal slow-cooker size: 4-qt.*

1 (14-oz.) package extra-firm tofu, pressed and cut into 1-inch chunks

1 Tbsp. olive oil

½ cup vegan vegetable broth

10 drops Frank's RedHot Sauce

2 Tbsp. coconut aminos

2 drops liquid stevia

2 tsp. flaxseed

1 medium onion, chopped

2 cloves garlic, minced

½ tsp. ground ginger

2 cups broccoli florets

1 medium red bell pepper, sliced

1. Brown tofu chunks slightly in oil in skillet. Place in slow cooker.

2. Stir in remaining ingredients.

3. Cover. Cook on High 1–1½ hours or on Low 2–3 hours.

Calories 171
Fat 10
Sodium 130
Carbs 10
Sugar 3
Protein 12

Sweet & Sour Garlic Honey Tofu

Maria Shevlin
Sicklerville, NJ

SLOW-COOKER

Makes 4 servings

Prep. Time: 20 minutes plus pressing time ⚘ Marinating Time: overnight ⚘
Cooking Time: 2 hours ⚘ Ideal slow-cooker size: 6-qt.

14-oz. block extra-firm tofu

Marinade:

2 Tbsp. vegetable stock

½ tsp. salt

⅛ tsp. pepper

1 Tbsp. garlic powder

1 Tbsp. Nature's Hollow Honey Substitute

1 tsp. coconut aminos

⅛ tsp. xanthan gum

½ yellow bell pepper, cut into cubes

1 medium onion, cubed

1½ cups frozen cut green beans

2 Tbsp. olive oil, *divided*

2 Tbsp. Alternasweets Low Carb Spicy Ketchup

2 Tbsp. Nature's Hollow Honey Substitute

5 cloves chopped garlic, browned lightly

1. Press the tofu.

2. Mix together all of the marinade ingredients and pour over tofu in an airtight container. Refrigerate and marinate overnight.

3. Sauté the bell pepper, onion, and green beans in a skillet over medium heat with 1 Tbsp. of the olive oil. Place contents into the crock.

4. Fry your tofu in the same skillet and brown lightly on all sides.

5. Drain on a paper towel then add to the crock.

6. Add in the ketchup, honey substitute, and garlic. Stir to lightly coat the tofu.

7. Cover and cook on Low for 2 hours.

TIP
If you don't already have a tofu press I recommend you get one. It helps so much when preparing any type of dish using tofu.

Calories 222
Fat 11
Sodium 380
Carbs 22
Sugar 13
Protein 11

Teriyaki Tempeh Steaks with Sugar Snap Peas

Hope Comerford
Clinton Township, MI

Makes 4–6 servings
Prep. Time: 10 minutes ⚜ Cooking Time: 5 hours ⚜ Ideal slow-cooker size: 5-qt.

3 (8-oz.) blocks of tempeh

I Tbsp. onion powder, *divided*

I Tbsp. garlic powder, *divided*

Salt to taste

Pepper to taste

I cup coconut aminos

15 drops liquid stevia

½ Tbsp. flaxseed

½ medium onion, sliced into half rings

1½–2 cups sugar snap peas

1. Place the tempeh blocks in your crock and sprinkle them with half the onion powder, half the garlic powder, and a bit of salt and pepper.

2. Mix together the coconut aminos, liquid stevia, and flaxseed.

3. Pour half of the coconut aminos sauce over the contents of the crock.

4. Place your onion slices on top and sprinkle them with more salt, pepper, and the rest of the garlic powder and onion powder. Pour the rest of the coconut aminos sauce over the top.

5. Cover and cook on Low for 5 hours.

6. About 40 minutes before the cook time is up, add in the sugar snap peas.

7. Serve the tempeh with some of the sugar snap peas on top and sauce from the crock drizzled over the top.

Calories 248

Fat 13

Sodium 1781

Carbs 14

Sugar 2

Protein 30

Asian Pepper Tofu

Donna Lantgen
Rapid City, SD

SLOW-COOKER

Makes 4 servings

Prep. Time: 20 minutes plus pressing time & *Cooking Time: 4 hours* & *Ideal slow-cooker size: 4-qt.*

1 (14-oz.) package extra-firm tofu, pressed and cut into strips

½ cup vegan vegetable broth

3 Tbsp. coconut aminos

1 Tbsp. coconut oil

½ tsp. ground ginger

1 garlic clove, minced

1 medium green pepper, thinly sliced

1 cup sliced fresh mushrooms

1 medium onion, thinly sliced

½ tsp. crushed red pepper

1. Combine all ingredients in slow cooker.

2. Cover. Cook on Low 4 hours.

Serving suggestion:

Serve over shirataki noodles and with fresh bean sprouts on top.

Calories 69
Fat 3
Sodium 369
Carbs 5
Sugar 1
Protein 8

Ginger Tempeh

Amy Troyer
Garden Grove, IA

Makes 4–5 servings
Prep. Time: 10 minutes ⚭ Cooking Time: 5 hours ⚭ Ideal slow-cooker size: 2- to 3-qt.

3 (8-oz.) blocks of tempeh, cut into 6 squares

1 large onion, sliced

2 bell peppers, sliced

2 tsp. ginger

15 drops liquid stevia

2 Tbsp. olive oil

½ cup liquid aminos

2 cloves garlic, minced

1. Place tempeh in slow cooker, and top with the sliced onion and peppers.

2. Mix together remaining ingredients.

3. Pour sauce over tempeh, onions, and peppers.

4. Cook on Low 5 hours.

Serving suggestion:

Serve over shirataki noodles or cauliflower rice.

Calories 330
Fat 20
Sodium 1075
Carbs 16
Sugar 2
Protein 31

Tasty Tempeh

Mary Puskar
Forest Hill, MD

Makes 4–6 servings
Prep. Time: 15 minutes ⚬ Cooking Time: 5 hours ⚬ Ideal slow-cooker size: 4-qt.

3 (8-oz.) blocks tempeh

3 Tbsp. olive oil

1 onion, sliced

1 green pepper, cut in strips

1 (8-oz.) can no-sugar-added tomato sauce

1½ Tbsp. Truvia Brown Sugar Blend

1 Tbsp. white rice vinegar

1½ tsp. salt

1 tsp. coconut aminos

1. Brown tempeh blocks in oil in skillet. Transfer to slow cooker.

2. Add remaining ingredients to cooker.

3. Cover. Cook on Low 5 hours.

4. Slice and serve over cooked cauliflower rice if desired.

Calories 294
Fat 19
Sodium 720
Carbs 13
Sugar 2
Protein 24

Garlic Tempeh

Earnie Zimmerman
Mechanicsburg, PA

Makes 6 servings
Prep. Time: 15–20 minutes   ❧   Cooking Time: 5 hours   ❧   Ideal slow-cooker size: 4-qt.

3 (8-oz.) blocks tempeh
1 Tbsp. vegan butter
1 tsp. salt
½ tsp. coarsely ground black pepper
1 medium onion, sliced
6 cloves garlic, peeled
8 strips (each 3-inch long, ½-inch wide) fresh lemon peel
1 head cauliflower, broken up
1 lb. celery sticks
½ tsp. dried thyme
1 cup vegan vegetable broth

1. Grease interior of slow-cooker crock.

2. If you have time, heat butter in 12-inch skillet over medium-high heat until hot. Place tempeh blocks in skillet and brown lightly on all sides.

3. If you don't have time, place tempeh directly into crock.

4. Sprinkle all over with salt and pepper.

5. In a large bowl, mix together onion, garlic, lemon peel, cauliflower, celery, and thyme. Stir in vegetable broth.

6. Spoon mixture into crock alongside and over the top of the tempeh.

7. Cover. Cook on Low 5 hours.

8. Slice tempeh into ½-inch-thick slices. Place on a platter. Serve topped with vegetables and broth.

Calories 265
Fat 14
Sodium 467
Carbs 16
Sugar 2
Protein 24

Savory Slow-Cooker Tempeh

Sara Harter Fredette
Williamsburg, MA

Makes 4 servings
Prep. Time: 25 minutes ⚜ Cooking Time: 5 hours ⚜ Ideal slow-cooker size: 4- or 5-qt.

2 (8-oz.) packages tempeh, each sliced into 2 pieces

I lb. fresh tomatoes, chopped, or I (15-oz.) can stewed tomatoes

I bay leaf

¼ tsp. pepper

2 cloves garlic, minced

I onion, chopped

½ cup vegan vegetable broth

I tsp. dried thyme

¼ tsp. salt

2 cups broccoli, cut into bite-sized pieces

1. Combine all ingredients except broccoli in slow cooker.

2. Cover. Cook on Low for 5 hours.

3. Add broccoli 30 minutes before serving.

Calories 278
Fat 13
Sodium 196
Carbs 20
Sugar 5
Protein 26

Main Dishes 133

Savory Tempeh Roast

SLOW-COOKER

Mary Louise Martin
Boyd, WI

Makes 4–6 servings
Prep. Time: 15 minutes ⚬ Cooking Time: 5 hours ⚬ Ideal slow-cooker size: 5-qt.

3 (8-oz.) blocks of tempeh
1 tsp. ground ginger
1 Tbsp. fresh minced rosemary
½ tsp. mace or nutmeg
1 tsp. coarsely ground black pepper
2 tsp. salt
2 cups vegan vegetable broth.

1. Grease interior of slow-cooker crock.

2. Place tempeh blocks into crock.

3. In a bowl, mix spices and seasonings together. Sprinkle half on top of the tempeh blocks, pressing them into the tempeh, then flip them over and sprinkle the rest on the other side.

4. Pour the vegetable broth around the edges, being careful not to wash spices off the tempeh.

5. Cover. Cook on Low 5 hours. Slice and serve.

Serving suggestion:

This would be good served alongside the Roasted Broccoli on page 161 or the Colorful Oven-Roasted Vegetables on page 197.

Calories 220
Fat 12
Sodium 652
Carbs 9
Sugar 0
Protein 23

Tempeh and Cabbage Dinner

SLOW-COOKER

Mrs. Paul Gray
Beatrice, NE

Makes 4–6 servings
Prep. Time: 25 minutes ⚭ Cooking Time: 5–6 hours ⚭ Ideal slow-cooker size: 4- or 5-qt.

3 (8-oz.) blocks of tempeh

¾ cup chopped onions

¼ cup chopped fresh parsley, or 2 Tbsp. dried parsley

4 cups shredded cabbage

I tsp. salt

⅛ tsp. pepper

½ tsp. caraway seeds

⅛ tsp. allspice

½ cup vegan vegetable broth

1. Place tempeh in slow cooker. Layer onions, parsley, and cabbage over it.

2. Combine salt, pepper, caraway seeds, and allspice. Sprinkle over cabbage. Pour broth over cabbage.

3. Cover. Cook on Low 5 hours.

Calories 240
Fat 12
Sodium 367
Carbs 13
Sugar 2
Protein 24

Herbed Tempeh

Sarah Herr
Goshen, IN

Makes 6 servings
Prep. Time: 20 minutes ⚭ Cooking Time: 5 hours ⚭ Ideal slow-cooker size: oval 6-qt.

3 (8-oz.) blocks tempeh

½ head cauliflower, broken/chopped into pieces

2 cups brussels sprouts

2 ribs celery, cut into small chunks

½ tsp. salt

½ tsp. dried rosemary

½ tsp. dried thyme

¼ tsp. garlic powder

¼ tsp. onion powder

¼ tsp. paprika

¼ tsp. coarsely ground pepper

3 Tbsp. vegan balsamic vinegar

1. Grease interior of slow-cooker crock.

2. Place tempeh in crock.

3. Place veggies around tempeh

4. Sprinkle herbs and spices evenly over all.

5. Drizzle balsamic vinegar over top.

6. Cover. Cook on Low 5 hours.

Calories 245
Fat 12
Sodium 194
Carbs 14
Sugar 2
Protein 25

Peppercorn Tempeh

Karen Ceneviva
Seymour, CT

Makes 6 servings
Prep. Time: 15–20 minutes & Cooking Time: 5 hours & Ideal slow-cooker size: 4- or 5-qt.

1–2 Tbsp. cracked black peppercorns
3 (8-oz.) blocks of tempeh
2 cloves garlic, minced
3 Tbsp. vegan balsamic vinegar
⅓ cup liquid aminos
2 tsp. dry mustard

1. Rub cracked pepper and garlic onto tempeh blocks, then place them in slow cooker.

2. Make several shallow slits in top of tempeh blocks.

3. In a small bowl, combine remaining ingredients. Spoon over tempeh.

4. Cover and cook on Low for 5 hours.

Calories 233
Fat 12
Sodium 595
Carbs 11
Sugar 2
Protein 25

Hungarian Tempeh with Paprika

Maureen Csikasz
Wakefield, MA

SLOW-COOKER

Makes 6 servings
Prep. Time: 15 minutes ⚭ Cooking Time: 5 hours ⚭ Ideal slow-cooker size: oval 5- or 6-qt.

3 (8-oz.) blocks tempeh

2–3 medium onions, coarsely chopped

5 Tbsp. sweet paprika

¾ tsp. salt

¼ tsp. black pepper

½ tsp. caraway seeds

I clove garlic, chopped

½ green bell pepper, sliced

¼ cup water

½ cup vegan sour cream

fresh parsley

1. Grease interior of slow-cooker crock.

2. Place tempeh blocks in crock.

3. In a good-sized bowl, mix all ingredients together, except sour cream and parsley.

4. Spoon evenly over tempeh.

5. Cover. Cook on Low 5 hours.

6. Cut into chunks or slices.

7. Just before serving, dollop with vegan sour cream. Garnish with fresh parsley.

Calories 276
Fat 16
Sodium 260
Carbs 16
Sugar 3
Protein 25

Vegan Pepper Steak-less

Maria Shevlin
Sicklerville NJ

Makes 4 servings

Prep. Time: 30 minutes plus pressing time ⚹ Cooking Time: 2 hours ⚹ Ideal slow-cooker size: 6-qt.

14-oz. block extra-firm tofu, sliced and pressed

3 cups diced bell peppers, various colors

1 medium to large onion, cubed

1 cup sliced mushrooms

2 stalks celery, cut on an angle

1 cup vegetable stock

1 Tbsp. coconut aminos or tamari

1 tsp. salt

½ tsp. white pepper

2 cloves garlic, minced

1 Tbsp. fresh parsley, chopped

¼ tsp. xanthan gum

Optional:

Shirataki rice (I use Better Than brand)

Green onions

Sesame seeds

1. Place the tofu, bell peppers, onion, mushrooms, and celery into the crock.

2. In a bowl, mix the vegetable stock, coconut aminos, and salt, white pepper, garlic, and parsley. Pour over the contents of the crock.

3. Cover and cook on High for 1 hour and then Low for 1 hour.

4. Remove ¼ cup of broth and mix the xanthan gum into it and pour the mixture back into the crock and stir well.

Serving suggestion:

Serve over shirataki rice and top with green onions and/or sesame seeds. The tofu gets very tender and flavorful in this dish.

Serving suggestion:

Toss with black or white sesame seeds.

Calories 107
Fat 4
Sodium 813
Carbs 8
Sugar 2
Protein 11

Four-Pepper Tempeh

SLOW-COOKER

Renee Hankins
Narvon, PA

Makes 14 servings
Prep. Time: 30 minutes ⚜ Cooking Time: 5–8 hours ⚜ Ideal slow-cooker size: 4- or 5-qt.

3 (8-oz.) blocks of tempeh, cut in ¼–½-inch-thick slices

1 yellow pepper, sliced into ¼-inch-thick pieces

1 red pepper, sliced into ¼-inch-thick pieces

1 orange pepper, sliced into ¼-inch-thick pieces

1 green pepper, sliced into ¼-inch-thick pieces

2 cloves garlic, sliced

2 large onions, sliced

1 tsp. ground cumin

½ tsp. dried oregano

1 bay leaf

salt to taste

2 (14½-oz.) cans low-sodium diced tomatoes

Jalapeño slices, *optional*

1. Place the sliced tempeh, sliced bell peppers, garlic, onions, cumin, oregano, bay leaf, and salt in slow cooker. Stir gently to mix.

2. Pour cans of diced tomatoes over the top. Sprinkle with jalapeño slices if you wish. Do not stir.

3. Cover and cook on Low 5 hours.

Serving suggestion:

Serve over cauliflower rice. Toss with cilantro just before serving.

Calories 124
Fat 5
Sodium 102
Carbs 11
Sugar 2
Protein 10

Slow-Cooked Pepper Tempeh Steak

Carolyn Baer
Conrath, WI

Ann Driscoll
Albuquerque, NM

Makes 6 servings
Prep. Time: 25 minutes ⚜ Cooking Time: 5 hours ⚜ Ideal slow-cooker size: 4-qt.

3 (8-oz.) blocks of tempeh, cut into 1-inch strips

2 Tbsp. olive oil

¼ cup coconut aminos

1 garlic clove, minced

1 cup chopped onion

5 drops liquid stevia

¼ tsp. pepper

¼ tsp. ground ginger

2 large green peppers, cut in strips

4 medium tomatoes, cut in eighths, or 1 (16-oz.) can diced tomatoes

½ cup cold water

1 Tbsp. flaxseed

1. Lightly brown tempeh slices in oil in saucepan. Transfer to slow cooker.

2. Combine coconut aminos, garlic, onion, stevia, pepper, and ginger. Pour over tempeh.

3. Cover. Cook on Low 4 hours.

4. Add green peppers and tomatoes. Cook 1 hour longer.

5. Combine water and flaxseed. Stir into slow cooker. Cook on High until thickened, about 10 minutes.

Calories 291
Fat 17
Sodium 458
Carbs 15
Sugar 3
Protein 26

Swiss Tempeh Steak

Hope Comerford
Clinton Township, MI

Makes 4–6 servings
Prep. Time: 20 minutes ⚗ Cooking Time: 4 hours ⚗ Ideal slow-cooker size: 6-qt.

3 (8-oz.) blocks of tempeh, cut into 6 pieces

⅓ cup almond flour

2 tsp. salt

½ tsp. pepper

3 Tbsp. vegan butter

I large onion, or more, sliced

I large pepper, or more, sliced

I (14½-oz.) can stewed tomatoes, or 3–4 fresh tomatoes, chopped

½ cup vegan vegetable broth

1. Sprinkle tempeh pieces with almond flour, salt, and pepper.

2. Lightly brown the tempeh pieces in butter over medium heat on top of stove. Transfer to crock.

3. Place the remaining ingredients into the crock.

4. Cover. Cook on Low 4 hours.

Serving suggestion:

Serve with mashed cauliflower.

Calories 367

Fat 23

Sodium 993

Carbs 21

Sugar 3

Protein 26

Side Dishes

Tabbouleh

Pat Bechtel
Dillsburg, PA

Makes 4 main-dish servings
Prep. Time: 10 minutes ⚬ *Marinating Time: 2 hours*

1 cup cooked cauliflower rice

½ lb. (about 2) fresh tomatoes, peeled and diced

½ cucumber, diced

4 green onions, white and green parts, minced

2 cups fresh blueberries

5 Tbsp. fresh lemon juice

¼ cup olive oil

½ cup shredded fresh mint leaves

1 Tbsp. chopped fresh parsley

¼ tsp. ground cumin

¼ tsp. salt

¼ tsp. freshly ground black pepper

1. Combine all ingredients in a large bowl, tossing gently.

2. Cover and refrigerate. Allow to marinate 2 hours before serving.

3. Serve at room temperature.

Calories 194
Fat 14
Sodium 138
Carbs 18
Sugar 10
Protein 2

Broccoli Salad

CHILLED

Elaine Vigoda
Rochester, NY

Makes 4 servings
Prep. Time: 15 minutes ⚓ Chilling Time: 1 hour

4 cups coarsely chopped fresh broccoli florets

½ cup finely chopped sweet Vidalia onion

3 Tbsp. white rice vinegar

¼ cup stevia granules

¼ cup olive oil

¼ cup Vegenaise Dressing and Sandwich Spread

I Tbsp. prepared mustard

½ cup vegan dry-roasted peanuts

1. Combine broccoli and onion in a large bowl.

2. In a separate bowl, whisk together vinegar, stevia, oil, Vegenaise, and mustard.

3. Toss dressing with salad.

4. Chill for 1 hour.

5. Add peanuts just before serving.

Calories 362
Fat 31
Sodium 297
Carbs 16
Sugar 7
Protein 8

Sesame Broccoli

Marci Baum
Manheim, PA

Makes 6 servings
Prep. Time: 10 minutes ⚹ Cooking Time: 10 minutes

1 head (about 6 cups) broccoli
1 tsp. sesame oil
1 Tbsp. sesame seeds
2 Tbsp. water
1 Tbsp. coconut aminos
¼ tsp. red pepper flakes, crushed
½ Tbsp. fresh lemon juice

1. Cut broccoli into small florets. Peel and dice stem and add to florets.

2. Heat a large skillet over medium-high heat. Pour oil into skillet and swirl to coat bottom. Cook sesame seeds for 1 minute, stirring constantly.

3. Stir in broccoli. Increase heat to high and cook 3 minutes, or until broccoli is bright green, stirring constantly.

4. Stir in remaining ingredients. Reduce heat to medium and cook, covered, 5 minutes, or until broccoli becomes crisp-tender.

Calories 21
Fat 2
Sodium 116
Carbs 1
Sugar 0
Protein 1

Roasted Broccoli

Andrea Cunningham
Arlington, KS

Makes 4 servings
Prep. Time: 10 minutes ⚭ Baking Time: 20 minutes

I head (about 5 cups) broccoli, cut into long pieces all the way through (you will eat the stems)

I Tbsp. olive oil

2–3 cloves garlic, sliced thin

Pepper to taste

Lemon wedges

1. Preheat oven to 400°F.

2. Place broccoli in baking pan with sides. Drizzle with olive oil. Toss to coat.

3. Sprinkle garlic and pepper over top.

4. Transfer to oven and roast 15–20 minutes, or until broccoli is crispy on the ends and a little browned.

5. Sprinkle with lemon juice.

Calories 71
Fat 4
Sodium 38
Carbs 8
Sugar 2
Protein 3

Broccoli and Bell Peppers

Frieda Weisz
Aberdeen, SD

Makes 8 servings
Prep. Time: 20 minutes ⚜ Cooking Time: 4–5 hours ⚜ Ideal slow-cooker size: 3½- or 4-qt.

2 lb. fresh broccoli, trimmed and chopped into bite-sized pieces

I clove garlic, minced

I green or red bell pepper, cut into thin slices

I onion, peeled and cut into slices

4 Tbsp. coconut aminos

½ tsp. salt

Dash black pepper

I Tbsp. sesame seeds, *optional* (as garnish)

1. Combine all ingredients except sesame seeds in slow cooker.

2. Cook on Low for 4–5 hours. Top with sesame seeds.

Calories 19
Fat 1
Sodium 460
Carbs 4
Sugar 1
Protein 2

Coleslaw

Bonnie Lahman
Broadway, VA

Makes 8–10 servings
Prep. Time: 25 minutes

I medium head cabbage, shredded

I red bell pepper, diced

I small onion, grated

I cup Vegenaise Dressing and Sandwich Spread

⅓–½ cup stevia granules

2 Tbsp. white rice vinegar

I Tbsp. Maille Dijon mustard

¼ tsp. salt

1. In salad bowl, mix cabbage, red pepper, and onion.

2. In separate small bowl, mix Vegenaise, stevia, vinegar, mustard, and salt.

3. Pour over cabbage mixture. Mix gently.

TIP
If you prefer a salad with less juice, add dressing just before serving.

Calories 87

Fat 7

Sodium 260

Carbs 6

Sugar 4

Protein 0

Homestyle Cabbage

Sandra Haverstraw
Hummelstown, PA

Makes 6 servings
Prep. Time: 20–25 minutes ⚸ Cooking/Baking Time: 30 minutes

I medium head cabbage

2 Tbsp. vegan butter

I Tbsp. stevia granules

I medium onion, thinly sliced

I medium green or yellow bell pepper, cut in thin rings

I (28-oz.) can diced tomatoes, or stewed tomatoes

½ tsp. salt

⅛ tsp. pepper

I cup vegan shredded cheddar cheese

1. Cut cabbage into 6 wedges, removing core.

2. Place cabbage in small amount of water in pot.

3. Cover. Cook 10 minutes. Drain.

4. Place in greased 9×13-inch baking pan.

5. In saucepan, melt vegan butter.

6. Add stevia, onion, and bell pepper rings.

7. Cook over medium heat until veggies are tender.

8. Add tomatoes, salt, and pepper. Stir.

9. Pour sauce over cabbage.

10. Bake at 350°F for 20–30 minutes.

11. Sprinkle with vegan shredded cheese during last 5 minutes of baking.

Calories 159
Fat 10
Sodium 507
Carbs 11
Sugar 3
Protein 6

Stir-Fry Cabbage

Esther Bowman
Gladys, VA

Makes 4–6 servings
Prep. Time: 10 minutes ⚬ Cooking Time: 15 minutes

2 Tbsp. vegan butter
I small onion, chopped
I clove garlic, minced
4 cups shredded cabbage
½ cup diced red pepper
⅛ tsp. paprika
I tsp. salt
Dash pepper
2 tsp. coconut aminos

1. Melt vegan butter in large skillet or wok.

2. Briefly stir-fry onion and garlic, then add cabbage and pepper. Stir-fry over medium heat about 5 minutes or until vegetables are tender-crisp.

3. Add paprika, salt, pepper, and coconut aminos and mix well. Serve at once.

Calories 59
Fat 4
Sodium 452
Carbs 5
Sugar 2
Protein 2

Brussels Sprouts with Pimentos

Donna Lantgen
Rapid City, SD

Makes 8 servings
Prep. Time: 10 minutes ⚬ *Cooking Time: 6 hours* ⚬ *Ideal slow-cooker size: 3½- or 4-qt.*

2 lb. brussels sprouts

¼ tsp. dried oregano

½ tsp. dried basil

2-oz. jar pimentos, drained

¼ cup, or 1 small can, sliced black olives, drained

1 Tbsp. olive oil

½ cup water

1. Combine all ingredients in slow cooker.

2. Cook on Low 6 hours, or until sprouts are just tender.

Calories 70
Fat 2
Sodium 60
Carbs 11
Sugar 3
Protein 4

Zucchini Ribbons

Delores Gnagey
Saginaw, MI

Makes 4 servings
Prep. Time: 15 minutes & Cooking Time: 9 minutes

I large zucchini, unpeeled, ends trimmed

I Tbsp. olive oil

3 cloves garlic, minced

I cup cherry tomato halves

½ tsp. dried basil

Pepper to taste

1. With vegetable peeler, slice zucchini into long, lengthwise strips, thick enough not to bend. (If strips are too thin, they'll get mushy while sautéing.)

2. Heat oil in large skillet over medium heat. Add zucchini ribbons. Sauté 4 minutes.

3. Add garlic and sauté 2 more minutes.

4. Add cherry tomatoes and sauté 2 additional minutes.

5. Sprinkle with basil and pepper to taste. Cook 1 minute.

Calories 43
Fat 4
Sodium 4
Carbs 3
Sugar 1
Protein 1

Fresh Zucchini and Tomatoes

Pauline Morrison
St. Marys, ON

Makes 6–8 servings
Prep. Time: 15 minutes ⚜ Cooking Time: 2½–3 hours ⚜ Ideal slow-cooker size: 3½-qt.

1½ lb. zucchini, peeled if you wish, and cut into ¼-inch slices

1 (19-oz.) can stewed tomatoes, broken up and undrained

1½ cloves garlic, minced

½ tsp. salt

1½ Tbsp. vegan butter

1. Place zucchini slices in slow cooker.

2. Add tomatoes, garlic, and salt. Mix well.

3. Dot surface with butter.

4. Cover and cook on High 2½–3 hours, or until zucchini are done to your liking.

Calories 51
Fat 2
Sodium 237
Carbs 6
Sugar 3
Protein 1

Pizza-Style Zucchini

Marcella Roberts
Denver, PA

Makes 6 servings
Prep. Time: 20 minutes ⚭ *Cooking Time: 2½ hours* ⚭ *Ideal slow-cooker size: 4-qt.*

2 medium zucchini, unpeeled and cut in disks

2 medium yellow squash, unpeeled and cut in disks

½ cup tomato sauce

¾ tsp. Italian seasoning

5 drops liquid stevia

½ tsp. garlic powder

½ tsp. onion powder

1 large tomato, diced

1 cup vegan shredded mozzarella cheese

sliced black olives, *optional*

1. Layer zucchini in lightly greased slow cooker, alternating colors.

2. Mix together the tomato sauce, Italian seasoning, liquid stevia, garlic powder, and onion powder. Stir in the tomato. Pour over zucchini and yellow squash.

3. Sprinkle with vegan shredded mozzarella and black olives (if using).

4. Cover and cook on High for 2 hours, until bubbly. Remove lid and cook an additional 30 minutes on High to evaporate some of the liquid.

TIP
Add basil, oregano, and chopped garlic if you want to really amp up the pizza flavor.

Calories 63
Fat 3
Sodium 215
Carbs 4
Sugar 215
Protein 5

Cucumber Salad with Cumin

Kim Patrick
Norwood, PA

Makes 6 servings
Prep. Time: 30 minutes

2 Tbsp. Vegenaise Dressing and Sandwich Spread

Juice of 1 lemon

Zest of 1 lemon

1 tsp. cumin seed, toasted

1–2 tsp. stevia granules

¼ tsp. sea salt

2 peeled cucumbers, seeded (if desired) and sliced

1. Whisk Vegenaise, lemon juice, lemon zest, cumin seed, stevia, and salt together.

2. Toss over sliced cucumbers.

Calories 48
Fat 3
Sodium 112
Carbs 4
Sugar 0
Protein 1

Marinated Sliced Tomatoes

CHILLED

Dawn Alderfer
Oley, PA

Makes 6 servings
Prep. Time: 10 minutes & Chilling Time: 3–12 hours

6 medium tomatoes, sliced

⅔ cup olive oil

¼ cup white rice vinegar

¼ cup minced fresh parsley

1 Tbsp. stevia granules

2 tsp. fresh marjoram, or ¾ tsp. dried marjoram

1 tsp. salt

¼ tsp. pepper

1. Place tomatoes in a large bowl.

2. Combine oil, vinegar, parsley, stevia, marjoram, salt, and pepper in a container with a tight-fitting lid. Shake well.

3. Pour over tomatoes. Chill for several hours or overnight, spooning dressing over tomatoes at least twice.

4. To serve, use a slotted spoon to lift tomatoes out of marinade. Lay on a platter.

Calories 245
Fat 24
Sodium 328
Carbs 7
Sugar 5
Protein 1

Tomato Salad

Ruth Fisher
Leicester, NY

Makes 12 servings
Prep. Time: 25 minutes   ✿   *Chilling Time: 3–4 hours*

6 ripe tomatoes, diced

3 sweet bell peppers, sliced (try a red, a green, and a yellow for color)

1 red onion, sliced thin

1 cup pitted black olives

⅔ cup olive oil

¼ cup apple cider vinegar

¼ cup fresh parsley

¼ cup chopped green onions

¼ tsp. pepper

2 tsp. sugar

¼ tsp. dried basil

1. Combine all vegetables in a large mixing bowl.

2. Mix remaining ingredients together in a separate bowl.

3. Pour dressing over vegetables. Mix thoroughly.

4. Cover and refrigerate 3–4 hours.

Calories 139
Fat 13
Sodium 88
Carbs 6
Sugar 0
Protein 1

Baked Tomatoes

Lizzie Ann Yoder
Hartville, OH

Makes 4 servings
Prep. Time: 10 minutes   ⚭   Cooking Time: 45 minutes–1 hour   ⚭   Ideal slow-cooker size: 2½- or 3-qt.

2 tomatoes, each cut in half

½ Tbsp. olive oil

½ tsp. parsley, chopped, or ¼ tsp. dry parsley flakes

¼ tsp. dried oregano

¼ tsp. dried basil

1. Spray slow-cooker crock with cooking spray. Place tomato halves in crock.

2. Drizzle oil over tomatoes. Sprinkle with remaining ingredients.

3. Cover. Cook on High 45 minutes–1 hour.

Calories 27
Fat 2
Sodium 3
Carbs 2
Sugar 2
Protein 1

Wild Mushrooms Italian

Connie Johnson
Loudon, NH

Makes 4–5 servings
Prep. Time: 20 minutes ⚓ *Cooking Time: 6–8 hours* ⚓ *Ideal slow-cooker size: 5-qt.*

2 large onions, chopped

3 large red, orange, or yellow bell peppers, chopped

3 large green bell peppers, chopped

2–3 Tbsp. olive oil

1 (12-oz.) package oyster mushrooms, cleaned and chopped

4 cloves garlic, minced

3 fresh bay leaves

10 fresh basil leaves, chopped

1 Tbsp. salt

1½ tsp. pepper

1 (28-oz.) can Italian plum tomatoes, crushed, or chopped

1. Sauté onions and peppers in oil in skillet until soft. Stir in mushrooms and garlic. Sauté just until mushrooms begin to turn brown. Pour into slow cooker.

2. Add remaining ingredients. Stir well.

3. Cover. Cook on Low 6–8 hours. Remove bay leaves and serve.

Calories 171
Fat 9
Sodium 410
Carbs 22
Sugar 10
Protein 5

Roasted Asparagus

Barbara Hoover
Landisville, PA

Makes 3–4 servings
Prep. Time: 10 minutes ☙ Baking Time: 10 minutes

1 lb. fresh asparagus
2 Tbsp. olive oil
2 tsp. sesame oil
¼ tsp. salt
¼ tsp. black pepper
1–2 Tbsp. sesame seeds

1. Trim any tough, woody stems from asparagus. Place asparagus on an ungreased large baking sheet.

2. Combine the olive oil and sesame oil in a small bowl. Spoon mixture over asparagus. Sprinkle with salt and pepper. Toss asparagus to coat and arrange in a single layer on the baking sheet.

3. Roast at 400°F until tender, about 10 minutes. Turn the baking sheet front to back and end to end halfway through roasting.

4. Meanwhile, toast the sesame seeds in a large skillet over medium heat, stirring constantly until golden, 1–2 minutes. Sprinkle seeds over roasted asparagus. Serve immediately.

TIP

For extra flavor, add 2 tsp. balsamic vinegar to olive and sesame oil in Step 2 before roasting.

Calories 108
Fat 10
Sodium 123
Carbs 5
Sugar 2
Protein 3

Stir-Fried Asparagus

Sylvia Beiler
Lowville, NY

Makes 6 servings
Prep. Time: 5 minutes ⚖ *Cooking Time: 2–3 minutes*

I Tbsp. olive oil
3 cups asparagus, sliced diagonally
4 green onions, sliced diagonally
I garlic clove, minced, *optional*
I tsp. lemon juice

1. Heat oil in pan. Add sliced vegetables.

2. Stir-fry until crisp-tender.

3. Sprinkle with lemon juice. Serve immediately.

Calories 37
Fat 2
Sodium 3
Carbs 4
Sugar 2
Protein 2

Lemony Garlic Asparagus

Hope Comerford
Clinton Township, MI

Makes 4 servings
Prep. Time: 5 minutes & Cooking Time: 1½–2 hours & Ideal slow-cooker size: 2- or 3-qt.

I lb. asparagus, bottom inch (tough part) removed
I Tbsp. olive oil
1 ½ Tbsp. lemon juice
3–4 cloves garlic, peeled and minced
¼ tsp. salt
⅛ tsp. pepper

1. Spray crock with nonstick spray.

2. Lay asparagus at bottom of crock and coat with the olive oil.

3. Pour the lemon juice over the top, then sprinkle with the garlic, salt, and pepper.

4. Cover and cook on Low for 1½–2 hours.

Serving suggestion:

Garnish with diced pimento, garlic, and lemon zest.

Calories 57
Fat 4
Sodium 123
Carbs 6
Sugar 2
Protein 3

Slow-Cooker Beets

Hope Comerford
Clinton Township, MI

Makes 4–6 servings
Prep. Time: 10 minutes ⚜ *Cooking Time: 3–4 hours* ⚜ *Ideal slow-cooker size: 3-qt.*

4–6 large beets, scrubbed well and tops removed

3 Tbsp. olive oil

1 tsp. sea salt

¼ tsp. pepper

3 Tbsp. vegan balsamic vinegar

1 Tbsp. lemon juice

1. Use foil to make a packet around each beet.

2. Divide the olive oil, salt, pepper, balsamic vinegar, and lemon juice evenly between each packet.

3. Place each beet packet into the slow cooker.

4. Cover and cook on Low for 3–4 hours, or until the beets are tender when poked with a knife.

5. Remove each beet packet from the crock and allow to cool and let the steam escape. Once cool enough to handle, use a paring knife to gently peel the skin off each beet. Cut into bite-sized pieces and serve with juice from the packet over the top.

Calories 103
Fat 7
Sodium 426
Carbs 10
Sugar 7
Protein 1

Colorful Oven-Roasted Vegetables

Kathy Bless
Fayetteville, PA

OVEN

Makes 10–12 servings
Prep. Time: 15 minutes ⚜ Baking Time: 45 minutes

5⅓ Tbsp. (⅓ cup) vegan butter, cut into chunks

½ tsp. dried thyme

¼–½ tsp. salt

¼ tsp. pepper

3 cups cauliflower florets

1½ cups sliced bell peppers

½ large onion, chopped

2 cups broccoli florets

1. Place butter in a 9×13-inch baking pan.

2. Place in oven set at 375°F to melt.

3. Stir in thyme, salt, and pepper.

4. Add cauliflower, peppers, and onion.

5. Toss to coat with butter mixture.

6. Bake at 375°F for 25 minutes. Stir.

7. Stir in broccoli florets.

8. Bake 20 minutes more, or until vegetables are tender-crisp.

Calories 60
Fat 4
Sodium 78
Carbs 6
Sugar 2
Protein 3

Green Beans with Tomatoes and Garlic

Shirley Sears
Sarasota, FL

Makes 6 servings
Prep. Time: 15 minutes ⚬ Cooking Time: 60–70 minutes

I Tbsp. olive oil

4 cloves garlic, chopped

I ½ lb. green beans, washed and stemmed

2 (8-oz.) cans crushed tomatoes, no salt added

I tsp. dried oregano

1. Heat oil in large skillet over medium heat.

2. Add garlic and sauté briefly.

3. Add beans and stir to coat with oil.

4. Add tomatoes.

5. Bring to a boil. Reduce heat to a low simmer.

6. Stir in oregano.

7. Cover and cook 45–60 minutes, or until beans are done to your liking and liquid is nearly absorbed.

Calories 90
Fat 3
Sodium 182
Carbs 15
Sugar 7
Protein 4

Lemon Garlic Green Beans

Dorothy Lingerfelt
Stonyford, CA

Makes 4 servings
Prep. Time: 10 minutes & Cooking Time: 10–13 minutes

2 cloves garlic, minced

2 tsp. olive oil

1 lb. fresh green beans, trimmed and broken in pieces

1 Tbsp. lemon juice

1 Tbsp. lemon zest

¼ tsp. ground pepper

⅛ tsp. salt

1. In large skillet, cook garlic in oil over medium heat for 30 seconds.

2. Add green beans.

3. Cook, stirring frequently, for 10–13 minutes, until as tender-crisp as you like them.

4. Stir in lemon juice, lemon zest, pepper, and salt.

Calories 58
Fat 3
Sodium 67
Carbs 9
Sugar 4
Protein 2

Herbed Green Beans with Tomatoes

Doreen Miller
Albuquerque, NM

Makes 6–8 servings
Prep. Time: 45 minutes ⚭ Cooking Time: 25 minutes

I garlic clove, minced

2 Tbsp. olive oil

⅓ cup thinly sliced green onions

I Tbsp. minced fresh basil, or I tsp. dried basil

I Tbsp. minced fresh oregano, or I tsp. dried oregano

½ tsp. salt

4 medium fresh tomatoes, peeled and chopped

4 cups fresh green beans cut into 2-inch pieces

I cup water

1. In a large frying pan, sauté garlic in olive oil for 1 minute. Do not allow to brown.

2. Add green onions, basil, and oregano. Cook a few minutes.

3. Add salt, tomatoes, green beans, and water. Cook uncovered until beans are as tender as you like them, 10–20 minutes.

Calories 66
Fat 4
Sodium 125
Carbs 8
Sugar 4
Protein 2

Desserts

CHILLED

Chocolate Mousse

Meg Suter
Goshen, IN

Makes 8 servings
Prep. Time: 10 minutes ⚜ *Cooking Time: 1–2 minutes* ⚜ *Chilling Time: 2–4 hours*

2 (12-oz.) bags Lily's Semi-Sweet Chocolate Baking Chips

1 (15-oz.) container silken tofu

1. Place chocolate chips in microwaveable bowl. Microwave in 30-second increments, stirring and checking each time until chocolate is melted.

2. Combine melted chocolate and tofu in a blender. Blend until smooth.

3. Refrigerate in serving bowl or individual glass dishes until well chilled. Serve.

Calories 436
Fat 26
Sodium 44
Carbs 56
Sugar 47
Protein 7

Lotsa Chocolate Almond Cake

Hope Comerford
Clinton Township, MI

SLOW-COOKER

Makes 10 servings

Prep. Time: 10 minutes ⚜ Cooking Time: 3 hours ⚜ Cooling Time: 30 minutes ⚜ Ideal slow-cooker size: 6-qt.

4 tablespoons flaxseeds

4 tablespoons water

1½ cups almond flour

18 packets stevia

⅔ cup unsweetened cocoa powder

¼ cup keto/vegan-friendly chocolate protein powder

2 tsp. baking powder

¼ tsp. salt

½ cup coconut oil, melted

¾ cup almond milk

1 tsp. vanilla extract

1 tsp. almond extract

¾ cup chopped 90% dark chocolate

1. Cover any hot spot of your crock with aluminum foil and spray crock with nonstick spray.

2. Combine flaxseeds and water and stir together.

3. In a bowl, mix together the almond flour, stevia, cocoa powder, protein powder, baking powder, and salt.

4. In a different bowl, mix together the coconut oil, flaxseeds and water, almond milk, and vanilla and almond extracts.

5. Pour wet ingredients into dry ingredients and mix until well-combined. Stir in chopped chocolate.

6. Pour cake mix into crock. Cover and cook on Low for 3 hours.

7. Turn the slow cooker off when the cooking time is over and let the cake cool in the crock for 30 minutes.

8. Place a plate or platter over the crock, then turn the crock upside down on the plate, so the cake releases onto the plate or platter.

Calories 426
Fat 32
Sodium 95
Carbs 31
Sugar 17
Protein 10

Black and Blue Cobbler

Renee Shirk, Mount Joy, PA

Makes 6 servings
Prep. Time: 20 minutes ⚸ Cooking Time: 2–2½ hours ⚸ Cooling Time: 30 minutes ⚸
Ideal slow-cooker size: 5-qt.

I cup almond flour

36 packets stevia, *divided*

I tsp. baking powder

¼ tsp. salt

¼ tsp. ground cinnamon

¼ tsp. ground nutmeg

½ cup silken tofu

2 Tbsp. almond milk

2 Tbsp. coconut oil, melted

2 cups fresh, or frozen, blueberries

2 cups fresh, or frozen, blackberries

¾ cup water

I tsp. grated orange peel

18 packets stevia

1. Combine almond flour, 18 packets stevia, baking powder, salt, cinnamon, and nutmeg.

2. Combine silken tofu, almond milk, and oil. Stir into dry ingredients until moistened.

3. Spread the batter evenly over bottom of greased slow cooker.

4. In saucepan, combine berries, water, orange peel, and remaining 18 packets stevia. Bring to boil. Remove from heat and pour over batter. Cover.

5. Cook on High 2–2½ hours, or until toothpick inserted into batter comes out clean. Turn off cooker.

6. Uncover and let stand 30 minutes before serving.

Calories 207
Fat 14
Sodium 165
Carbs 21
Sugar 8
Protein 6

Raspberry Almond Bars

Phyllis Good
Lancaster, PA

Makes 24 servings
Prep. Time: 20–30 minutes ⚜ *Cooking Time: 2½–3 hours* ⚜ *Ideal slow-cooker size: 6-qt. oval*

1 ½ cups almond flour

¼ cup flaxseed

12 packets stevia

8 Tbsp. vegan butter, softened

½ tsp. vegan almond extract

½ cup Good Good Sweet Raspberry Jam

⅓ cup sliced almonds

TIP
Watch for the raspberry jam to ooze out around the edges as these bars bake!

1. Grease interior of slow-cooker crock.

2. In a large bowl, combine flour, flaxseed, and stevia.

3. Cut in butter with a pastry cutter or two knives—or your fingers—until mixture forms coarse crumbs.

4. Stir in extract until well blended.

5. Set aside 1 cup crumbs.

6. Press remaining crumbs into bottom of crock.

7. Spread preserves over crust to within ½ inch of the edges (the preserves could burn if they touch the hot crock).

8. In a small bowl, combine reserved 1 cup crumbs with almonds. Sprinkle evenly over jam, pressing down gently to hold the almonds in place.

9. Cover. Cook on High for 2½–3 hours, or until firm in center.

10. Uncover. Lift crock onto wire baking rack to cool.

11. When room temperature, cut bars into 20 squares and 4 triangles in the corners.

Calories 89
Fat 2
Sodium 28
Carbs 4
Sugar 0
Protein 2

SLOW-COOKER

Berries Jubilee

Hope Comerford
Clinton Township, MI

Makes 4 servings
Prep. Time: 15 minutes ⚭ *Cooking Time: 3–4 hours* ⚭ *Ideal slow-cooker size: 2-to- 3-qt.*

I lb. fresh cherries, pitted

¼ cup erythritol

I tsp. lemon juice

I tsp. lemon zest

I tsp. vanilla extract

⅓ cup rum

2 Tbsp. water

2 Tbsp. flaxseed

1. Spray crock with nonstick spray.

2. Place cherries in crock with erythritol, lemon juice, lemon zest, vanilla, and rum.

3. Mix together the water and flaxseed, then stir this into the contents of the crock.

4. Cook on Low for 3–4 hours.

Calories 254
Fat 3
Sodium 6
Carbs 52
Sugar 11
Protein 4

Crispy Tofu with Toasted Coconut and Warm Strawberry Compote

Maria Shevlin
Sicklerville, NJ

Makes: 2–4 servings
Prep. Time: 25 minutes plus pressing time & Cooking Time: 15 minutes

14-oz. block extra-firm tofu
1 cup strawberries, diced
1 tablespoon vegan butter
12 tablespoons sweetener
2 Tbsp. coconut oil
½ cup coconut flakes

Serving Suggestion:
Would also be delicious served with homemade coconut whipped cream.

1. Press tofu to remove moisture.

2. Add the diced strawberries to a pan with vegan butter and sweetener. Cook about 10 minutes on low, stirring often. Set aside. This is your compote to use when serving.

3. Cut tofu into cubes.

4. Fry in coconut oil until browned and lightly crisp.

5. Place tofu on plate with paper towel to drain oil.

6. In another pan add the coconut flakes and toast quickly, then remove from pan.

7. Place a few pieces of the crispy tofu into a sundae dessert cup, add coconut flakes, then add 1–2 tablespoons of the strawberry compote.

8. Layer 1–2 more times if desired.

Calories 330
Fat 16
Sodium 57
Carbs 37
Sugar 31
Protein 11

Metric Equivalent Measurements

If you're accustomed to using metric measurements, I don't want you to be inconvenienced by the imperial measurements I use in this book.

Use this handy chart, too, to figure out the size of the slow cooker you'll need for each recipe.

Weight (Dry Ingredients)

1 oz		30 g
4 oz	¼ lb	120 g
8 oz	½ lb	240 g
12 oz	¾ lb	360 g
16 oz	1 lb	480 g
32 oz	2 lb	960 g

Slow-Cooker Sizes

1-quart	0.96 l
2-quart	1.92 l
3-quart	2.88 l
4-quart	3.84 l
5-quart	4.80 l
6-quart	5.76 l
7-quart	6.72 l
8-quart	7.68 l

Volume (Liquid Ingredients)

½ tsp.		2 ml
1 tsp.		5 ml
1 Tbsp.	½ fl oz	15 ml
2 Tbsp.	1 fl oz	30 ml
¼ cup	2 fl oz	60 ml
⅓ cup	3 fl oz	80 ml
½ cup	4 fl oz	120 ml
⅔ cup	5 fl oz	160 ml
¾ cup	6 fl oz	180 ml
1 cup	8 fl oz	240 ml
1 pt	16 fl oz	480 ml
1 qt	32 fl oz	960 ml

Length

¼ in	6 mm
½ in	13 mm
¾ in	19 mm
1 in	25 mm
6 in	15 cm
12 in	30 cm

Recipe & Ingredient Index

About the Author

Hope Comerford is a mom, wife, elementary music teacher, blogger, recipe developer, public speaker, Young Living Essential Oils essential oil enthusiast/educator, and published author. In 2013, she was diagnosed with a severe gluten intolerance and since then has spent many hours creating easy, practical and delicious gluten-free recipes that can be enjoyed by both those who are affected by gluten and those who are not.

Growing up, Hope spent many hours in the kitchen with her Meme (grandmother) and her love for cooking grew from there. While working on her master's degree when her daughter was young, Hope turned to her slow cookers for some salvation and sanity. It was from there she began truly experimenting with recipes and quickly learned she had the ability to get a little more creative in the kitchen and develop her own recipes.

In 2010, Hope started her blog, *A Busy Mom's Slow Cooker Adventures*, to simply share the recipes she was making with her family and friends. She never imagined people all over the world would begin visiting her page and sharing her recipes with others as well. In 2013, Hope self-published her first cookbook, *Slow Cooker Recipes 10 Ingredients or Less and Gluten-Free*, and then later wrote *The Gluten-Free Slow Cooker*.

Hope became the new brand ambassador and author of Fix-It and Forget-It in mid-2016. Since then, she has brought her excitement and creativeness to the Fix-It and Forget-It brand. Through Fix-It and Forget-It, she has written *Fix-It and Forget-It Lazy & Slow, Fix-It and Forget-It Healthy Slow Cooker Cookbook, Forget-It Cooking for Two, Fix-It and Forget-It Instant Pot Cookbook, Fix-It and Forget-It Freezer Meals*, and many more.

Hope lives in the city of Clinton Township, Michigan, near Metro Detroit. She's a native of Michigan and lived there her whole life. She has been happily married to her husband and best friend, Justin, since 2008. Together they have two children, Ella and Gavin, who are her motivation, inspiration, and heart. In her spare time, Hope enjoys traveling, singing, cooking, reading books, spending time with friends and family, and relaxing.

Also Available